# So, You've Accepted Jesus:

## A New Believer's Starter Kit

# So, You've Accepted Jesus:

## A New Believer's Starter Kit

**Andrew D. Sargent, Ph.D.**

**&**

**Amy S. Kinder, M. A.**

This book is dedicated to the young woman to whom I was trying to witness on the streets of New York City in the summer of 1987 (whose name I've long forgotten) for chastising me for using "Christianese" and being unable to explain exactly what I meant by certain words and phrases when she asked me to. Her challenge that I learn to clearly explain why the cross of Christ works to forgive sins changed the course of my life as a Christian, a preacher, and a scholar. Thank you, and I hope you found Jesus in spite of my youthful blundering.

~Andrew

I'd also like to Thank Amy Kinder, my co-author in this work, for so much help well beyond the portions she penned. Her conversations and critiques, advice and encouragement were deeply appreciated.

# Meet the Authors

### Amy S. Kinder, M.A.:

Amy has a Master of Arts in Old Testament Studies from Ashland Theological Seminary (2006 ) and a Bachelor of Arts in Biblical Studies from Northpoint Bible College (2001). She currently serves at Real Church in Ohio as the Discipleship and Teaching Pastor where she has developed the Real Institute that offers classes for new believers and those looking to deepen their knowledge and personal study of the Bible. She has a passion for inviting others to seek a deeper relationship with God by mingling insightful biblical teaching with raw stories of humanity. Amy is not afraid to tackle difficult subjects in the pursuit of authentic applications of God's Word to the messiness of life.

### Andrew Sargent, Ph.D.:

Andrew Sargent has a Ph.D. in Theology with an Old Testament concentration from Trinity International University (2010), A Master of Arts in Old Testament Studies from Gordon-Conwell Theological Seminary (2002), and a Master of Arts in Biblical Studies from Regent University (1997). He is the founder and President of Biblical Literacy Ministries (1998-present), and Assistant Pastor at Sacred Fire Church in Belleview Florida. His passion is training leaders at every level of ministry in proper Biblical Interpretation methods, helping them discover the joys of biblical theology, biblical languages, and the often ignored historical, cultural, and literary backgrounds to Scripture in the Ancient Near Eastern world.

# Table of Contents

.

# Introduction

If you've read Andrew's book with Jonathan and Britney Cashman, *Go! Making 21st Century Disciple Makers,*[1] you know that he has a deep interest in helping new believers get locked into a Church family and launching them on the road of becoming disciples of Jesus Christ in the fullest sense of the phrase. Over the years, We've encountered a lot of questions from new believers and made unofficial catalogues of the kinds of things that take them by surprise when they first begin attending church services. Most, if not all of them are touched upon here, but we have also added a few discussions that address matters about which we wish new believers *would* inquire.

Our goal is to be five things: Informative, personal, entertaining, mentoring, and brief. We have been informed that 1000 words a day is not generally regarded as being brief when those 1000 words introduce subjects for consideration that virtually demand their own book... and a nearby dictionary. Far from the average daily devotional of today (but not so far afield from those of bygone days), we go well beyond fluffy thoughts for a quick uplift, and lay tracks for meaningful development as true disciples of Christ. We hope you find enough depth here to warrant coming back again and again to hash over the deepening implications that these short lessons can have for you as you grow to be more and more "in love" with Jesus. Not the creepy, "Jesus is my boyfriend love," but the deep devotion that comes with increasing admiration and a desire to imitate and emulate greatness.

Andrew has been told by certain professors that humor and sarcasm are unbefitting a scholar. Well, all he can say is, "All the worse for scholarship." We hope the levity will lighten the burden of some of the messaging. This book gives a panoramic picture of the possibilities that lay before you as you continue your travels with Jesus. The breadth of that consideration can be overwhelming, especially if the "demands" of discipleship come one after the other like speeding motorists when you are trying to run across a sixteen lane highway at rush hour. I don't know why you'd be fool enough to try this, but I can easily understand the feeling. One day the devotional will you to examine your life in terms of various forms of addiction that may need address, and the next day be prodded to develop a lifestyle of prayerfulness. I get it. You are not expected to master the things discussed herein, so much as to have them put on your radar, but still... it can be a lot to take in. Just breathe.

---

[1] Jonathan and Britney Cashman & Andrew Sargent, Ph.D., *Go! Making 21st Century Disciple Makers,* 2016.

So, if a month seems too much too fast, you may want to dedicate a few days to each discussion, perhaps a week, rereading, spending some time with the scriptures the lesson touches upon, meditating on the implications that it has for your personal journey, keeping a journal of your thoughts, challenges, and insights as you go. We'll give some guiding questions and some space to write if you need a little.

We have prayed for you as we wrote these lessons, and we wish you all the joy and peace that Jesus has brought to our own lives.

~Andrew & Amy

# DAY ONE
## So You've Accepted Jesus

If you recently responded to an invitation to "accept Jesus as your savior," or "prayed the sinner's prayer" with someone telling you about Jesus, let me welcome you to the Christian family.[2]

That said… and earnestly meant… today, you may think of me as that quirky In-law who pulls you aside the first time you meet the rest of the family, seeking to discover the true depth of your commitment and to let you know what you're in for with a clan like ours.

> Tip: Every group develops a special language whether it's a baseball team, a company, philosophical tradition or religion. Christianity is no exception. We have a lot of words, phrases, and practices that will come naturally to you faster than you imagine. Just remember to ask for insider information when you encounter something you don't understand. I won't say that there is no such thing as a stupid question, I've been teaching long enough to know there is, but don't worry about it. In my experience, Christians are pretty gracious and won't laugh at you to your face… and I'm sure that snickering behind the Pastor's office door has nothing to do with you.

As suggested above, becoming a Christian is a little like getting married. You join yourself for life to the most important person you will ever meet—Jesus Christ[3]—and suddenly find yourself with a big family. Some of them are great, and, to be honest, some are a little weird. God loves the weirdoes, and I'm glad He does… because, some people think I'm one of them. You'll have to judge that for yourself by the end of this book.

Part of the rewarding struggle of a marriage is discovering your beloved and your beloved's family and facing these and other challenges together as they come to you over years. Remember the immortal words of the great non-prophet Miley Cyrus, "It's the climb!" This whole book of devotions is designed to present a panoramic picture of being Christian, of being part of the Christian family… our special vocabulary, our perspectives and values, some of our religious practices… not head shaving and itchy robes, but stuff like taking communion, getting baptized, praying, worship, giving, and stuff like that.

---

[2] Even if you've been a Christian for a while, don't stop reading; there is a lot in these pages that may benefit you as well.

[3] Christ is not Jesus' last name; it's His title. It means that he is the fulfillment of the ancient promises given to the nation of Israel that God would send them an anointed ruler like King David, David's own son, who would fulfill all the promises of God for them as a people. He did come. His name is Jesus, He was God in the flesh… what we call incarnate God.

Just as it would be a mistake when getting married to panic over the dark possibilities in life before they even materialize, you don't want to panic over the issues raised here. I mean to give you direction and purpose and forewarning, and hope we don't scare you with too much information too soon. Being Christian is a marathon not a sprint, and God's grace will provide the strength and wisdom you need, when you need it, if you seek Him for it.

So let's start at the beginning.

People become Christians when they wake up to God revealed in Jesus Christ, see the great offense that stands between them and God, and repent of living life away from God, of living in indifference to His right-of-place in their life as their Creator, of living in defiance of His loving commands in both heart and practice. They know that nothing that they could possibly do can compensate for their offense, but also discover that through the loving self-sacrifice of Jesus, Christ has purchased a pardon and paved a path back to God on the believer's behalf.

Our first step when once waking up to Him is usually to pray a prayer[4] of repentance[5]... telling God from an honest heart that we want to turn back from the corrupt path we've been traveling and to journey instead on His path, the path of life that He made as a blessing to us, and to make us a blessing to others. Holy God full of love responds to such genuine confessions with grace, and mercy. He forgives and begins the long work of transforming us to become more like Jesus.

That earnest prayer is a commitment to follow Jesus who has made provision for that forgiveness through His death on the cross. The wages of sin is death, but Jesus' sacrifice satisfies that Holy Justice on our behalf as we become members of His spiritual family. He, the perfect man, incarnate God, stands for us before the Holy courts and says, "That sinner there, is forgiven, he/she is with me."

That prayer anticipates our ongoing transformation to become more and more like Jesus as we strive for the discipline and wisdom to live in obedience to God's Word —The Bible. It is a promise that, with His help, we will join in His work of saving souls and making disciples. We call this "The Great Commission." It means telling people about Jesus, what He's done for us, and helping them start their own relationship journey with Him.

This is one of those things you shouldn't freak out about ahead of time. It's no weirder than telling your friends about a cool movie you think they'll like, or how much you love your new Keurig K-1500... except it actually matters.

---

[4] Prayer is communicating with God. It doesn't have to be flowery or fiery, just honest. Of course, other people who may be listening will find flowery and fiery a bit more entertaining, but since we aren't talking to them but to our Heavenly Father who loves us, they can lump it.

[5] Repentance is not penitence. Different word. Different idea altogether. Penitence involves punishing ourselves for our sins to earn something from God. Repentance simply means recognizing our error, and turning away from it to live a different life making different kinds of choices.

This moment of confession and repentance and gracious embrace by Christ is… so to speak… "the wedding," the point of promise, the moment of commitment to do life together with Jesus your Lord and Savior, and, thus, with other believers as well.

The marriage, however, is found in the decades of actually doing life together, where we "work out our salvation" in what the Scriptures call "fear and trembling."[6] Not terror, though it is a "fearful thing to fall into the hands of the living God,"[7] but respect tinged with an awed awareness of what it means to be in relationship with the Holy One through Whom all things have been made. We will falter and fail, but rise again through His grace and our ongoing repentance, reaching ever further to be transformed into His likeness. Christians should want to be like their hero.

~Andrew D. Sargent, Ph.D.

---

[6] Philippians 2:12, in the New Testament.
[7] Hebrews 10:31 in the New Testament.

# Reflections & Responses

Think about your own decision to follow Jesus. Describe your experience?

Where were you and how did you know that it was time to surrender your life to Jesus? What impact has this decision had on your life so far? We call this is your testimony, and the Bible tells us there is great importance in the word of our testimony, in part, because your personal experience with God and what Jesus has done for you on the cross can help others relate to Jesus as well. We recommend practicing your story. When you have is just right, perhaps write it here.

# DAY TWO
## Putting on Christian Glasses

Now, I know that Christians have a reputation for being the most stylish people in the room, but the title of our little chat today isn't about wearing fashionable eye-wear, though I'm more than happy to give you some tips. Here's one; monocles are out right now.

What the title "Putting on Christian Glasses" means is that being a believer in the God of the Bible should change the way you see the world; it should change the entire story that your heart preaches to you about the nature of the world in which you live… like putting on the right pair of glasses after decades of suffering with some untreated blur in your natural vision, or even of wearing the wrong pair of glasses.

In 1 Kings 18, we have a popular story in which the great prophet of Yahweh,[8] Elijah challenges the priests of the storm god Baal to a contest of deity—The winner answers prayer with fire and proves himself true god. In verse 21, Elijah makes the famous announcement, *"How long will you go limping between two different opinions? If Yahweh is God, follow him; but if Baal, then follow him."*

The wording here seems slight to the English ear, a wavering between two opinions as if Yahweh or Baal is chocolate or vanilla, Coke or Pepsi, Star Wars or Star Trek. Choose! This couldn't be further from reality. The nature of the contest is a contest between two worldviews, a contest between two radically different perceptions of reality, of the nature of time, the limits of human beings, the possibilities for human society, the character of law and order and the future of the human soul. No aspect of life is left untouched by it. It speaks to morality and ethics, reason and philosophy, purpose and meaning.

If Baal is god, then the entire system of paganism is true, humanity has no meaning, time is taking the world nowhere, the individual came from nothing and is going to nothing and nothing that he or she does in the interim has any real purpose. If Baal is god, then outcomes are not primarily decided by moral and ethical choices, but rather by the ritual manipulation of pagan gods. These gods are presented as short-sighted, petulant, and ego-maniacal. They get up to all sorts of mischief as they perpetually torment humanity… on purpose. If Baal is god, then humans are on their own in a universe without meaning. (Sounds a lot like Atheism!)

---

[8] Yahweh is the personal and covenant name chosen by God in Scripture. It comes from the Hebrew word YHWH which is a word of "Being." As spelled, it means "The Creator." He is the uncaused-cause of all that is. You will hear this name on occasion in Church so you may as well learn what it means now.

If Yahweh is God, however, then everything is different...
EEEVVVERYTHING!!!!!!

I don't know how old you are, Dearest Believer, and to be honest, I'm just too polite to ask, but if you were born after 1980, there is a better than average chance that the worldview you absorbed from society had more in common with the one believed by those Baal worshippers than the one preached by the Prophet Elijah. Western Civilization was imperfectly built on a deepening Biblical story about God, Man, and Reality, but a growing atheist view of reality has been waging war against it from within for centuries and has now taken root and dominates Millennials and GenZ.

In answer to the questions, "Where did you come from?" "What are you?" "What's wrong with the world?" and "How can the world be fixed?" two whole generations have been nurtured on humanism and answer these questions like atheists would. The atheist answers, apart from a thin veneer of scientism (not real science) look more than a little similar to the answers of old world pagans who, like them, sacrifice their children to the gods for the promise of a little more prosperity... a little more security.

Even those who claim to believe in God have embraced the central points of humanism—man is morally autonomous... i.e. free to do as he pleases... that truth is found within as "my truth." Moral goodness is measured in the thrall of passions, in the heat of wanting whatever it is that they want... sex, the same sex, to be a different sex, money, power, control. Love is assessed in moments of arousal—"Love is Love—If it feels good do it." This is a destructive short-game which defines freedom as freedom from restraint and freedom to do as one pleases, freedom to create one's own reality and the right to demand that others honor that confession. Would you call it freedom for the astronaut to cut his tether to the craft in outer space? In a moral sense, these do. They celebrate the path of death and call it freedom.

Man is not his own master, however. Truth is not within us, something of our own declaring. We each stand before One Holy Creator of all, owing Him everything. The world is His for He made it. We stand there as His special creation, made in His image, and endowed with all the rights and responsibilities of that status. We stand before Him amid a sea of His beloved creatures, being called to love them like He loves them.

Our primary purpose in life is to wake up to Him, to strive to be like Him, imitating His character and participating in the fulfillment of His purposes in the world. He has revealed all this to us in Holy Scripture... the Bible. We strive to be free FROM our own destructive passions and desires, our own selfishness, so that we can be free TO fulfill our purpose as His special creation whom He loves beyond measure. Our freedom is the freedom TO discover and walk on the path of life that He has laid before us for our blessing and others' benefit.

Put on those glasses. It may take time to wrestle through your own thoughts about God, Man, and Reality, but strive for that corrective. "Let God be true and every man a liar."[9]

These glasses aren't always fashionable, but they reveal truth, meaning, and purpose.

~Andrew D. Sargent, Ph.D.

---

[9] Romans 3:4 in the New Testament.

# Reflections & Responses

In what ways has Jesus helped you see the world from a different vantage point? What are some things you firmly believed before you came to know Jesus as your savior that you now see were in error?

How has this shift impacted your life so far? How has that change the way you act or behave?

What are some aspects of life that you're not seeing through "Christian Glasses," things in life and perhaps the Bible that you are having a hard time understanding?

Ask the Lord to show you HIS way of seeing that area in the Bible. Write down and date the scriptures you find about it. If you gain wisdom in this area, come back and tell the story here.

# DAY THREE
## Nice Guys Finish First

When my daughter and her other senior teammates ran their last track race together, they held hands and crossed the finish line together, shouting, "The class of 2008 Rules!" It was a beautiful moment.

The coach, however, hung his head, both smirking and bemoaning the display. Even though they took all the top spots of the race *en masse*, the judge stripped them of their placements and awarded their points to the other team pulling up the rear. Nice guys finish last, right?

In a selfish world, "Nice guys finish last" is an anthem to cruelty and trickery on the road to success because, there, success is measured through short-game thinking about the satisfying of greed and passions, and the quelling of fear in the accumulation and securing of stuff. There, "whoever dies with the most toys wins," however you define "toys."

According to Scripture, however, the ideal Christian assesses life differently; I call this Kingdom Accounting, because, in God's Spiritual Kingdom, success is declared by other measures. Ask my daughter about that loss and she beams with pleasure. It was a moment of solidarity between those who had shared much over their four years together, a glimmering crown of comradery. In fact, she is prouder of that moment than of all the wins over all those years of competition.[10] Just so, in Kingdom Accounting, "nice guys" finish first.

I'm being a tad playful with my use of "nice guys." Kingdom Accounting means measuring the value of things according to God's perspective. It isn't about being "nice," so much as being loving, and we must never mistake being pleasant and soft for being loving. Love seeks the good of others and, sometimes, because we live in a world populated with sinners like you and I, that demands some pretty unpleasant things.

You have to play a long-game when trying to determine what does and doesn't actually do good. Sometimes we have to choose between conflicting desires and warring parties. People tend to respond to incentives of personal gain, loss, pain and pleasure, but it is often hardship, struggle, self-denial and suffering that rewards us best in becoming the people God wants us to be, so that we do the work God wants us to do.

---

[10] This is not an attack against competition, for healthy competition does great good for the markets and for the whole of humanity through healthy markets. This is a recognition that there is more to life than outmaneuvering others to get what you want for yourself. Fair play, honestly, integrity, kindness, charity, and even losing at times have rewards that the selfish soul will never reap.

So as we move on, I want to give you a bird's eye view of what it means to be a Christian in practical terms. Far from requiring shaved heads,[11] itchy brown robes, and plain food, the Christian journey is one of finding and walking the path of life that God laid out for us in His creation. Finding and walking this hard-but-joyous road entails devotion to Jesus Christ in prayer, worship, and Bible study, but honestly, it has been my experience that 80-90% of being a disciple of Jesus is striving to become a genuinely good person. Walking on hot coals not usually required.

Now, we shouldn't assume going in that we already know what it means to be a good person, though most foolishly think they do, which is one of the reasons we need prayer, worship, and Bible study. A good portion of what ails us as human beings can be diagnosed in the fact that we are not truly good people, even when society tells us we are, and that we need God to teach us how to be. This is hard in a time when we are being inundated from every direction with messages telling us that being a good person means having no expectations for certain mascot groups... never making anyone feel bad about themselves or about what they do—(so long as what they do is sin—and that it is good and kind to accept whatever nonsense others declare to be good about themselves without challenge.

Rather, to do good means to cause good when that good is judged by long-term outcomes not short-term feelings or the deceit of immediate results. Disciplining a child does not please the child, but it secures the significant natural benefits of being a disciplined person. So too, the happiness of instantly gratifying childish wishes leads down a road of ultimate misery.

Life-long stability is important, but the eternal state of the soul is the ultimate long-game.

This principle applies broadly, whether it is misguided charity that does more harm than good, or strict morals that pain the wanton, but bring life and joy to the practitioner... or the criminal justice system where governmental brutality against evil doers increases the safety, order, and prosperity of society. Scripture tells us plainly that love "does not rejoice in unrighteousness, but rejoices with the truth."[12] And goodness can start there in knowing that we do not have "your truth" and "my truth" but THE TRUTH. So here is a panoramic of Christian discipleship.

- Desire the good of others and seek God to know what that looks like. It will seldom include poking them in the eyes and kicking their shins, but some may feel like you have when you speak truth to their lies.
- Focus on your responsibilities for doing good in every relationship you have.

---

[11] Mine is a fashion statement forced by nature.
[12] 1 Corinthians 13:6 in the New Testament.

- If you are a child of living parents, honor them. It's not always easy, and can be fraught with weird complications, but ask God how.[13]
- If you are a spouse, love them and study and pray about what that looks like in your situation.
- Do you have children? Raise them to find the path of the life that God has laid out for them in the world into eternity.
- Do you have neighbors? Bless them; pray for them; seek their good.
- Seek good for the waiter; be a blessing to the checkout girl; respect those in authority in any given situation.
- You are a citizen; be a good one. Obey the law. Respect other people's rights. Give an informed vote, and seek the good of your community, even if it requires resisting unjust governance. This is not a contradiction, but a tension, and a lesson in wisdom.

Ask yourself today, "In my life, which of these needs is crying out the hardest right now?"

~Andrew D. Sargent, Ph.D.

---

[13] A friend of mine's mother was a practicing witch and allowed others to sexually abuse him as a child. We talked earnestly of how he could honor his mother in her aged hour of need, without exposing his own children to her evil.

# Reflections & Responses

Humans easily distort their conceptions of love through selfishness. It is vital therefore, for Christians to relearn what, or rather who, love is. Read 1 Corinthians 13; 1 John 4, Philippians 2:1-11, & Romans 13:8-10, then take a few moments to prayerfully reflect on the true essence of love in action.

Describe some meaningful differences between what our culture tells us about love, and how God's word describes love. List some specific ways that this contrast challenges you to love differently?

# DAY FOUR
## The Forgiven Forgive
## Or
## I Can't Forgive, but I Must Forgive

If I compare myself to the most wretched people I can think of, I look pretty good. Faithful husband, even before getting married, lived a mostly honest life, only stolen two objects… both before 17.

But, I know a little of my inner man, and God knows the whole of me. On my own, before God, I would provoke a storm of holy fire that would consume me in everlasting judgment. If not for the grace and mercy that has come to me through the covering work of Jesus Christ, I'd be a 5'10.5" charcoal briquette almost indistinguishable next to Stalin's 5' 5" one.

In Luke 7:36-50, Jesus gets invited to dinner at the house of a religious leader who denies him all the common niceties of being a guest. While there, a woman of ill-repute gets into the house and falls weeping at Jesus' feet, which stick out behind Him as He sits on the ground at the table. She cleans His feet with her own tears, dries them with her hair, and anoints them with precious ointment. After illustrating with a story, Jesus tells the offended Rabbi, who is disgusted by Jesus' tolerance of such antics from 'that sort of woman,' "I tell you, her sins, which are many, are forgiven—for she loved much. But he who is forgiven little, loves little."

It is a matter of perception. When we understand just how great our offense against God was when Jesus forgave it, our love for God will be great, our gratitude beyond measuring, our humility plain to all. If, however, we see our sin as slight, (which it is not) as if a mere trifle for God to reasonably overlook, then our love for God and our gratitude for His mercy will be trivial, and our love of ourselves and our confidence in what we have to offer God will be great. Both are a precarious place to be.

The latter is beyond repentance until he comes to see himself reflected hideously back to himself in the holiness of God. The former has experienced a level of mercy that needs to be reflected back upon all those whom he or she has reason to resent, or even hate.

In Matthew 18:21-34, Jesus tells the parable of a man who owes his lord tens of billions in today's dollars and receives mercy when he begs for it. Then that forgiven servant goes out and finds a guy who owes him a couple months wages. He demands payment, chokes him out, and turns him over to debtor's prison when he can't cough it up. This does not sit well with the merciful lord, so he un-forgives the debt and casts that wicked sinner into debtor's prison. Jesus ends with some terrifying words for those of us who have been injured, robbed, offended, or even oppressed and struggle finding the ability or willingness to forgive. He says, "So also my heavenly Father will do to every one of you, if you do not forgive your brother from your heart."

Forgiveness can be a tricky word. In a meeting that my university class had with a famous Jewish Nazi hunter, one of my mates asked him, why don't you just forgive them? A look of puzzlement came over the man's face. He said, "God can forgive them at the end of a rope if He wishes, but it is my job to put them there." My associate was horrified by the reply. Each completely missed the fact that they were giving two different meanings to the word "forgive."

Men can forgive debts that are owed to them, but only God can forgive sins, because, ultimately, sin is against God. Still, people do wrong one another and owe debts that even Jesus will describe as "your brother sins against you." And it is this understanding of debt and forgiveness that we must cultivate. This distinction is lost on many, but Jesus is careful to tack on "from your heart" to "forgive" for this very reason.

The forgiveness that we extend as Christians is NOT a forgoing of justice. Criminal evil doers must be brought to justice if for no other reason than to keep them from continuing to do harm. Neither does the forgiveness that we extend depend on the repentance of those who've wronged us, nor on our ability to confront them… perhaps they are dead, unknown, or beyond reach. Forgiveness does not mean that you have to restore relationship with harmful individuals, or become door mats that refuse to hold others accountable for their actions. We may forgive people for what they've done, but we must deal with what they are doing, remember what they are, and never enable their ability to continue in evil.

The forgiveness that Jesus asks of those whom He has forgiven is to relinquish in our hearts the emotional debt that we believe others owe us for wrongs committed against us. It means that we stop cultivating revenge fantasies. It means that we stop mentally rehearsing their sins and nurturing our pain and anger over them. The forgiveness that Jesus asks is to release hate, to be healed from the damage that hate does to the hater. We need to stop acting out against others in one way or another, even innocents, because of that hate. One wise one has described unforgiveness as letting those who hurt you continue to hurt you by letting them live rent free inside your head. Another has noted that unforgiveness is like drinking poison in the hopes that the person who did you wrong will die.

Forgiveness is a process that begins, not ends, with deciding that you want to forgive, that for your own Christian growth you must forgive. So let's start there.

Pray, "Lord, I can't forgive, but I must forgive. You have forgiven the unforgivable in me; help me do the same for others."

~Andrew D. Sargent, Ph.D.

# Reflections & Responses

Take a few minutes and come before the Lord with gratitude for the mercy and forgiveness He has extended to you in Jesus. Think about his goodness towards you. List a few points of gratitude.

Now search your heart for areas that you might be wrestling with forgiveness towards someone who has wronged you.

Detail how our discussion of love (from our previous day's devotion) and forgiveness from today's might help you take steps to forgive? If this still seems like a struggle, ask the Lord to reveal His forgiveness of you more fully so that you might find the grace needed to forgive those in your own life.

# DAY FIVE
## Christians Worship God

If you've spent your life in church as I have, the special vocabulary of church as well as the common events of Sunday gatherings are like a comfy old blanket from childhood… washed of course. If, however, you are new to the entire idea of church, our terms and many of our doings must seem strange to you. Probably as strange as "going clubbing" is to me. Sorry I just don't get it.

A few years ago a group of friends started faithfully attending our church in Massachusetts. They kept to themselves in the back… up in the balcony… slipping in late… slipping out early. When the senior pastor finally found out who they were and got ahold of some of them to try to get to know them and to hear their story, they had some explanations for their "odd" behavior. They were new believers and, although they enjoyed our services, they were puzzled why we "wasted so much time singing." The preaching made sense to them, but our weekly spiritual hootenanny seemed a squandering of their precious minutes. So they came in late, got a sermon, and left as soon as the pastor concluded to avoid any Jesus-shindig that might break out at the end.

We decided that some sermons on worship were in order, because we weren't "wasting time singing." We were worshiping Jesus. Christians worship.

Weorthscipe is not a popular brand of Norwegian mouth wash, as one might think, but is the Old English origin of the word worship, which means "to ascribe worth." Worship is worth-ship, showing honor to that which is honorable, reverence for that which is revered.

In this sense, worship is any right-honoring response by people to what God is or what God does. So, if I recognize that God is Holy and respond to this holiness by dedicating myself to His purposes, that is a form of worship. If I respond to God's love for the hurting by reaching out a hand of help to them, then my charity becomes an act of worship. If I recognize that all that I have comes from Him and respond to this knowledge by paying tithes to His Church, then my giving become an act of worship.

So, back to our singing. Christians sing in church because they are practicing the most obvious sense of worship; they are praising God for who He is, thanking Him for what He's done, and reaching to Him to connect with His presence as they meditate through song on Him. Prayer and celebration and gratitude and spiritual communion all blend together in the heart of the singer standing together with the congregation before God, before Christ, ascribing honor and worth and glory and power and dominion to Him… not just over the world that He made, but over we who sing His praises together.

Worship is not a new-fangled invention by the Church to give artsy types like musicians, poets, and song writers something to do in the church service.

Humans have known since ancient days that music, poetry, and singing have a special place in the human experience, a profound impact on heart and soul. Hence, the old saw, "Music calms the savage beast." This, of course, brings us back to "clubbing," proving that only some music calms the savage beast, and raises our awareness of concerts and radio stations, CDs, streaming services and the like.

We live on love songs and love poems and find in them our own heart's desire for human connection. They put words to our feelings and rhythm to our longings. We use them to commune with or reach out to another on a special level. Think of the myriad of scenes in romantic comedies and ancient plays where the would-be lover serenades at the window. We find Romeo there courting his Juliette, and Cyrano de Bergerac speaking from the shadows. There too, we find drunken idiots like Ben Foster's character in *Get Over It*, belting out an off tune appeal for love from the girl who jilted him... and let's not forget young John Cusack holding his boom box over his head as it plays "Your Eyes" by Peter Gabriel in the famed, *Say Anything*. We know adoration, and we know that music and poetry and singing is a powerful expression of that emotion... that's why the whole audience sings along with Neil Diamond when he lyrics love to his "Sweet Caroline." Hold a flaming lighter over your head, lift your cell phone flashlight high, for we are moved to serene meditation by the shared experience of sweet songs.

There are, however, better songs to sing, better things over which to serenade, a better object for our devotion. This is worship.

One whole book of the Bible, indeed, the longest book of the Bible, called *Psalms*, is dedicated to the poetry of worshipping Hebrew prophets, inspired by the Holy Spirit in their celebration of God. They meditate on his goodness, stand in awe of His power, and even give voice to trust in the midst of sorrow and struggle. They teach the congregation in song how to worship the Creator "in Spirit and in truth."[14]

Christians are worshippers. They should hardly be able to contain the impulse. But sometimes they need instruction, and they need to step out in faith to cultivate the practice... not unlike children who need to be taught to say please and thank you, and, in learning to do so, become all the more mindful of respect and gratitude.

Christians are worshippers. Try it. You'll be glad you did.

~Andrew D. Sargent, Ph.D.

---

[14] John 4:24.

# Reflections & Responses

Take time today to search for Christian worship songs and hymns in places like Youtube music, Spotify, Apple music, Amazon music or Pandora. Take the time to record here a few songs that impact you in terms of your impulse to worship God, and that affect your thoughts about God.

Pick a song that you find particularly meaningful at this time in your life and listen to it several times, until you can catch the tune and sing along. (You don't have to sound good, but bathroom tiles add a bit to our tunefulness). Leave a record here for your future self discussing the song and why it impacts you especially at this time in life.

# DAY SIX
## Christians Break Addictions…
## 'cept Coffee… and Xbox

The goal of this series of devotions is to provide a panoramic view of Christianity. We are introducing, but certainly not encapsulating, a host of issues that face those who have spiritually bent their knee to the Lordship of Jesus Christ. Some of these will discuss special language, like "covenant" or church experiences like "Communion." Others, like this one, bring the need for behavioral changes into view… Christians aren't supposed to steal or lie or cheat or be sexually immoral.

Today, I'd like to bring up a matter that those who are serious about serving Jesus Christ must confront sooner or later… preferably sooner. Christians are called upon to break addictions. To say that Jesus is Lord and, yet, to struggle with impulse control over any number of destructive behavioral patterns or life controlling substances creates an innate tension. How can I be Christ's and become the person He wants me to be and do the work He wants me to do if my first love or first obedience is to life destroying and family destroying addictions?

The understanding of addiction is in constant flux, being heavily influenced at times by philosophical commitments to excuse destructive behaviors by casting addicts as victims of disease rather than as people who are morally or ethically compromised… those lacking discipline. Whatever the cause, it behooves Christians to break addictions so that it is they themselves and not some substance or "thrill" that controls their lives as they strive to walk in obedience to Jesus Christ.

I'd like to address a few points here.

First, the very nature of the way God made our brains leaves us susceptible to behavioral "addictions." The brain rewards us for certain types of "social" behaviors by creating chemicals that make us feel good. It can, however, be tricked into rewarding us for anti-social behaviors that look to the brain like socially advantageous behaviors. Whereas I was rewarded with dopamine by my brain in my youth for shoveling my elderly neighbor's driveway after a snow storm, today I can get the same kick from earning a hundred digital gold coins from Wordscapes for doing nothing more than being "awesome" with words. The clink of those glistening beauties as they fly into my treasure chest and make the numbers climb gets me every time and convinces me that no matter what my wife thinks, that was an hour well spent.

Second, some are more prone to compulsive behaviors than others. This is not an excuse, but it should generate some empathy. Growing up, my mother warned me and my siblings that we came from a long line of addicts and compulsive bad boys, and that we needed to be careful what footholds we gave the Devil. I took heed, and have, thus far, remained free from the typical list of life destroying addictions like smoking (*Stinky*), drugs (*Can't stand being mentally diminished*), alcohol (*Yuck & Diddo*), gambling (*I'm too cheap*) and wanton sexuality (*Tie me to the mast on this one!!!*).[15] I am keenly aware, however, that an addict lives in my skin just waiting for me to slip up… for me to give him an opportunity.

Me? McDonald's breakfasts will be the end of me, and Dr. Pepper has a Ph.D. in deliciousness!

Third, context is king. Unless it is a particular point of pride for the dying,[16] those late stage days of cancer agony is not necessarily the time to ride the high horse on pain meds and addiction fears. As one who has had major surgeries, I can attest that real (as opposed to the psychologically induced pain of addiction unmet) needs attention. There are many treatments for chronic pain that don't involve addictive substances, however, and we should always be wary of our propensity to addiction.

Fourth, some addictions are more destructive than others, but we should still take heed of the very idea of compulsive and addictive behaviors. Smoking is less damaging than Heroine, for instance, but it can still kill you and make you smell bad. Shopping binges may not ruin your marriage like drunkenness can, but it can still ruin your finances and diminish your ability and willingness to be generous with the money over which God has made you a steward.

And let's be honest, a coffee addiction denied will make you cranky, maybe leave you a little sleepy, and give you a big headache, BUT, it's not likely going to have you robbing strangers, or selling off the family TV to get yourself a fix. And let's not forget that it smells awesome and has the best memes on Facebook. So, you'll have to judge its impact on your life and effectiveness for yourself.

Other seemingly innocent behaviors need to be monitored for the impact that they have on our ability to be the people God wants us to be… especially with our families. Technology addictions, addictions to things to which technology gives easy access, video games, and uncontrollable TV binging can easily rob us of healthy social interactions. Junk food can make us fat (*trust me*) and diminish both the time and the quality of the time that we have with loved ones.

Scott Adams ran a powerfully insightful comic strip, where Dilbert asks Dogbert, "You know that good feeling that you get when you first put a Q-tip in your ear? Can I really enjoy it, or is it a sin?" Dogbert says, "I think it's okay."

---

[15] It ruins a joke to explain it, but here we go. In *Ulysses*, Odysseus has himself tied to the mast of his ship so he can sail through the dangerous territory of the Sirens who lure men to their deaths with their seductive song.

[16] I fear the idea that in some altered state as I lay dying I might embarrass myself and disparage my witness. Then I remember too, that tormenting pain can also drive a person to indecent words and acts.

Dilbert says, "Good, because I used a whole box yesterday." And there it is. Anything that controls us or diminishes us in our usefulness to our families or Jesus Christ needs attention… even if it's something cool like hunting or fishing.

You don't answer to me, but you should answer to Christ. Examine yourself, therefore, and, if need be, make a list of the things that you need to address. Ask God to bring conviction where wisdom is needed, and seek His help in setting yourself free for His service.

~Andrew D. Sargent, Ph.D.

# Reflections & Responses

We all have a bent toward compulsion & addiction of one sort or another. Spend a few moments evaluating your life and discuss some areas that might have more control over your behavior, mindset, or life than is healthy.

List some of your go-to comforts, or self-soothing behaviors. Describe the impact that each has on your life? Are any of these things that God might be nudging you to remove from your life? Ask the Lord for wisdom to recognize and reign in destructive or even distracting patterns that compete with Christ for supremacy in life.

# DAY SEVEN
## Christians Pray

Growing up we had a local store called Ann & Hope; it was like a flea market in a barely-converted penitentiary, but with less ambiance. Great deals though. Local Christians would joke, "Why go to Ann & Hope when you can go to God and pray?" My inner four year old laughs every time.

I grew up praying. I heard so much praying as a child that I started categorizing prayers by method, favorite phrases, and vocal patterns. We had powerful prayers that inspired, but also gossip prayers, where one wondered if the intent was seeking divine aid, or making sure that everyone knew about so & so's shenanigans. We had teaching prayers, reminding God about such & such a passage with lots of commentary. Many prayed in King James English and expanded my vocabulary with phrases like, "Know ye," and "Doest Thou." I discovered that "words proceedeth," and that "men smiteth." We had the "Father-God" prayers who replaced every pause with… well… you know… "Father-God."

So, as you might imagine, prayer doesn't seem weird to me in the least. All the good guys in the Bible prayed. Jesus prayed. Jesus even gave His disciples a beautiful pattern for prayer, which has been turned into more than a few inspiring songs… usually called either *The Lord's Prayer*, or *Our Father*.[17]

Prayer comes naturally to me… feeling, at times, only a little more intentional than thinking. I live life before the Lord, who knows the number of hairs on my head,[18] and the thoughts and intents of my heart.[19] He hears,[20] which is one of the benefits of being omniscient and omnipresent. He knows what I want before I ask,[21] but likes to be asked, and always reserves the right to respond for His purpose and my good, rather than satisfying my often misguided wishes.

The Apostle Paul instructs us to "pray without ceasing,"[22] which means remaining in open-channel conversation with God. So, pour out your concerns to Him, because he cares for you.[23] Seek His guidance.[24] Hold out others before

---

[17] Matthew 6:9-13. My favorite versions use the composition by Albert Hay Malotte. Look it up and take a listen. Jackie Evancho does a nice version… So does Andrea Bocelli and believe it or not, Reba McEntire.

[18] The fact that it is easier to count them on my head than your head does not take away from the miracle in the least… so stop laughing.

[19] Romans 8:26-27.

[20] Luke 11:9-13.

[21] Matthew 6:8.

[22] 1 Thessalonians 5:16-17.

[23] 1 Peter 5:6-7.

[24] John 16:13.

Him for special care, salvation, healing, and deliverance from troubles.[25] He is present with us… we should act like it. It's more than just therapeutic; it is one of the primary means by which God transforms us into the people He wants us to become, so that we can do the work He wants us to do.

My wife and I took a cruise to Alaska.[26] Each night we had dinner with a different set of vacationers. One 16 year old boy bred and trained mules. I saw a grand chance to answer the many questions I've always had about mules. (*Yes, I did have many previously unmet curiosities about these strange creatures.*) That's my way. I wanna know all that I can know about everything there is to know. I take my data where I can get it. Almost everyone can teach me something.

Then it struck me special one day; I am in communication with the Holy Creator of all. I have God, His Word, and His Holy Spirit to instruct, empower, convict, and guide. 2 Peter 1:3 says it perfectly. *His divine power has granted to us all things that pertain to life and godliness, through the knowledge of him who called us to his own glory and excellence.* James 1:5 provides an excellent follow, *If any of you lacks wisdom, let him ask God, who gives generously to all without reproach, and it will be given him.*

So Christians pray. They strive to keep open channels of communication with God. Their striving, of course, is not with God, Who is eager to commune with them.[27] Their striving is with themselves. They must learn to turn the echo chamber of their own self-talk into an open conference with the Lord of All Creation. This is a help in imitating Paul's own determination to "take every thought captive" so that He might obey Christ.[28] We must learn to consider God in all our dealings and reach out to Him consciously in word and thought as we navigate the complex world around us. Christians pray.

This, thus far, is the soul of prayer, but it doesn't stop there. Couples pray together. People pray for one another… sometimes in person. Christians also engage in group prayer and public prayer. Jesus warned His disciples about the lure of praying for the benefit of being seen, heard, and admired in Matthew 6:5-6, but prayer is still a legitimate and regular part of Christian gatherings. We pray with thanksgiving before eating, for protection before events and travels, for guidance before meeting or speaking. We pray for the sick and suffering in our services. We open in prayer, close in prayer, and pepper each transition with prayer whether seeking a blessing over the offering, participating in communion, or closing our time of worship. Christians pray.

Lastly, Christians cultivate the spiritual discipline of daily devotional prayer. This is often done upon waking so as to begin each day with our minds set on God. We take a short time to read the Bible, maybe a devotional thought

---

[25] 1 Timothy 2:1-2.

[26] It was beyond wonderful. It was a daily National Geographics special. I highly recommend it.

[27] Indeed, 2 Chronicles 16:9 tells us plainly that *"the eyes of the LORD run to and fro throughout the whole earth, to give strong support to those whose heart is blameless toward him."*

[28] 2 Corinthians 10:5.

by people who write books like this… perhaps we sing a song of worship, and then move through a series of prayer points for which there are many schemes. I like the old A.C.T.S. prayer. Adoration; confession; thanksgiving, and finally, supplication… which means seeking good things from God's hand.

Try it. It just may change your life.

~Andrew D. Sargent, Ph.D.

# Reflections & Responses

Try the A.C.T.S form of prayer today. Write some of it out here. Let's begin with Adoration – make the first part of your prayer thinking something about what makes God unique – how big He is, how powerful He is, how loving He is, how holy He is. Thank Him for this part of His character and express to Him the positive ways you see it impact your life and/or the world around you.

Confession – make this part of your prayer a time of confession of your own personal sins. Yes, we are indeed saved from our sins, but on this side of heaven, we will still sin. Our salvation doesn't make us perfect and we must still daily come before God with a repentant heart seeking His forgiveness for our shortcomings.

Thanksgiving – take a few minutes to thank God for anything and everything. Practicing gratitude will go a long way in shaping your new life and character in the ways of Christ. He will keep teaching you to be grateful in all things.

Supplication – now take the last few minutes of your prayer time to bring your needs and requests to the Lord. He loves you and wants to hear and meet your needs, as well as your requests on someone else's behalf.

# DAY EIGHT
## Reading the Bible & Loving It

Practicing Jews and Christians are called to be "people of the book." That doesn't mean they always are, but it does mean that while our religion is meant to be a relationship with our Creator through which we strive to become more and more like Him, we also believe that our Creator revealed Himself, His plan, and His purposes in the book we call Scripture. After nearly four decades as a biblical scholar, having read much of what has been written to discredit the Bible, I am even more convinced today that the Bible has been inspired by God than when I was growing up believing what my parents taught me about it.

The Bible is the most important and influential book in human history... most read... most translated... most quoted... most studied... subject of the most books.

It was penned by more than 40 authors over a period of some 1500 years. These authors were not born to the great civilizations; they were not the learned of world empires. They were born at the least likely of times in the least likely of places. They were shepherds and builders and farmers, and even those who became great, did so because of God, not from great opportunities that fell to them by birth. The one thing they all had in common was a conviction validated by fulfilled prophecy that the One Holy Creator of All had revealed Himself to them and that their writing was inspired by His Holy Spirit. They changed the world for unimaginable good, benefiting multiplied billions.

If God exists, which I believe the evidence demands, then He is a creator. If He is a creator, He is a communicator for He has made a world that preaches the Creator's power and glory, and cells encoded with His messaging, and proclamations about paths of life and death through the cause-effect structures in nature so that those who desire good can find it. We might think of things like the principle of sowing and reaping or even laws of causation.

The folly of children reveals the need for all of us to discover truth not INSIDE ourselves, riding our feelings like an ill-fated surfer, but OUTSIDE ourselves, discovering by observing God's world things like which berries will kill us and which will sustain us, how wheat grows best, and what kind of behavior leads to human thriving and which squanders human productivity.

If the Creator is a communicator, then we should expect Him to reach out to His creatures, even if for specific reasons, which we will discuss another time,[29] He does so through intermediary means rather than directly.

---

[29] God is omnipotent (all powerful) but chose to permit freedom of choice for His creatures so that love would be real. For love to be real it must be chosen amid options, not necessarily chosen without consequence. In short, a direct revelation of God would overwhelm human will, eliminating choice, and rendering devotion no more than irresistible mechanics.

In the entire history of man, no collection of books has done more to elevate the human race out of poverty, out of oppression, out of misery than Scripture. No work has done more than the Bible to teach men trustworthy patterns for family, society, and justice... all while preaching grace, mercy, and compassion. It stands head and shoulders over every other sacred text in areas of morality, ethics, love for one's neighbor, and even love for one's enemy. It is the reason for the rise of global literacy and public education.

After ages in stagnation, humanity began to rise at unprecedented speed and in incalculable ways once Scriptural influence began to spread across the globe, giving birth to the scientific method, free market economics, constitutional republics, the expansion of philosophy, the industrial age, and eventually the technological explosion. Economists call this rapid change the hockey stick of prosperity.... a long flat handle with a sharp upward turn at the blade. This upward turn did not come to everyone all at once, however, but only when any given people embraced basic principles from the West that the West got from the Bible. Without Scripture, the whole human race would still be trapped in the long ages of pagan dysfunction, for it alone shattered paganism's stranglehold on humanity, taught the people of many lands that there is a path of life to be found in the Creator's world, and, then, gave them the map to it.

Imagine such a treasure in your hands. What should one do with such a gift?

It's a book. Read it.

On Christmas morning, 1974, at the age of seven, my wife, Melodie, received her first adult Bible. She remembers no other gift from that year, though her parents were generous with their children and well-off. As she unwrapped it, and realized what it was, she describes herself as being awash with the sober importance of the moment, filled with awe and a little fear. She was holding responsibility in her hand, the map of the paths of life and death, knowing all the while that part of her inclined toward wanton ruin and another to divine order and blessing.

Me, I got army guys.

Even so, by 19, I was so spiritually hungry for biblical wisdom and knowledge that I wished that I could just eat the Bible like the Prophet Ezekiel did[30] and absorb it into my very being. Easy attainment, however, is not God's way. I've had to work at it, sacrificing my time and my energy and my arrogance to sit at the feet of God, learning from His prophets in His inspired Word.

The Christian life is not a 50 yard dash, so don't act like it is one by freaking out over how much there is to do. Being Christian is a marathon of many years of steady going, periods of exhilaration, periods of struggle, loss, and energizer-bunny growth... just keep going. Today, I want to call you to the

---

[30] Ezekiel Chapter 3 in the Old Testament.

love of God's Word. If you don't read it you can't learn from it. If you don't love it, you won't learn from it, even if you do read it.

~Andrew D. Sargent, Ph.D.

# Reflections & Responses

There is no greater resource to know and understand our lives before God as Christians than studying the Bible. If you aren't sure where to start, purchase a Bible – start with an ESV or NIV; they are easier to read. If you can't afford one, most churches are happy to give you one. You can also find reading plans on several different Bible apps like the YouVersion Bible app or the Life Bible App, which can be helpful guides as you are beginning to create a habit of reading God's Word daily.

If you don't know where to start – start in the book of Psalms (it's right in the middle of your Bible), Proverbs (it has 31 chapters, so it is perfect to read a chapter a day – it comes right after Psalms), Genesis chapters 1-11 (it's the first book of the Bible), and read through Luke and Acts (these are found in the New Testament).

Don't worry about what you don't know yet, just start reading! Write down your questions, trust me you will likely have questions for the rest of your life – it's actually a really beautiful thing about the Bible!

Remember, God isn't scared of your questions, and any Bible loving Christian (friend, leader, or pastor) would love to help you find answers and help you wrestle with your questions.

As a starting exercise, try reading the first few Psalms. Write down any questions that come to mind here, and ask your church's pastor for some help with them. Come back and write the answers here too.

# DAY NINE
# What to Expect
# When You're Expected to Read Your Bible

In my early teens, I tried to read the letters of Paul in the New Testament. It was an embarrassing experience. I lacked the skills to follow his arguments, had no context for the letter, and didn't understand the vocabulary. My reading interests at the time topped out at Sunday Comics and Encyclopedia Brown mysteries, which I forced my little brother to let me read to him. He never did thank me.

So, I'm the last person to imagine "Read your Bible!" is an easy ask. Most Scriptures are understandable to the average reader, but even Peter, one of Jesus' disciples, referred to some of the writings of "our beloved brother Paul" as "hard to understand."[31] Thanks, Saint Pete, my 13 year old self feels better.

Even so, it is important for Christians to become students of Scripture. If you attend the right kind of church, you will learn some Bible. If you attend Sunday School, you will learn yet more. Nothing, however, replaces reading the Bible again and again.

Before you rush for a Bible to start your journey, I'd like to at least prepare you a little bit for what you'll find there. It's good to have your head on straight when starting.

The Bible breaks into two major pieces. The Old Testament and the New Testament. I hope I don't have to say which comes first. Some of the material, though powerful to those who understand it, may freak you out a bit, or bore you to tears. Some needs informed discussion. I'll post warnings.

The Old Testament has collections of creation stories, history, law, worship, wisdom, and Prophetic sermons, some of which predict the fulfillment of God's salvation plan and tell people how they should think and act as they wait for that plan to fully unfold.

First we have "The Pentateuch," which is a hoity-toity word for the first five books: Genesis, Exodus, Leviticus, Numbers, and Deuteronomy.

Genesis (*needs informed discussion, but reads fine*) tells stories about creation, mankind's sin, the flood, the tower of Babel, and the call of Abraham into covenant relationship with God. This sets the stage for God's salvation plan. Genesis follows Abraham's son Isaac, Isaac's son Jacob/Israel, and Jacob's 12 sons, especially Joseph. It follows them from Mesopotamia to Canaan (The land promised to Abraham and his seed... errr Children) and on into Egypt where they go to escape a famine.

---

[31] 2 Peter 3:16 in the New Testament.

Exodus tells how Moses brings this group, called Hebrews and Israel, out of Egypt years later to prepare them for that Promised Land. It also details the new covenant that God makes with them which includes laws to live by (*need informed discussion*) and the construction of a place of worship (*May bore to tears*).

Their worship was a type of symbolic preaching. It revealed their need for salvation and God's special provision for it. Thus, the book of Leviticus gives many details about how these sinful people could live in the presence of a Holy God (*All warnings at once*).

Numbers tells stories about the Israelites before they enter into the Promise Land (*The first 10 chapters are challenging, may bore to tears*). Deuteronomy gives a second version of the Covenant and its laws just before they enter the Promised Land (*needs informed discussion but reads well*).

Then we have a series of preaching history books. Joshua tells about Israel's entrance into the Promised Land. Judges details the consequences of their often failed struggle to keep their covenant with God. In the books of Samuel, Kings, and Chronicles, we find the stories of Israel under Kings from the rise of the first to the devastation under the last. In between, we meet great characters like David, Solomon, Hezekiah, and Josiah. The Book of Ruth, tells the wonderful story of David's godly grandmother. (*The first 9 chapters of Chronicles will bore to tears… all genealogy.*)

Because of Israel's disobedience, God allows them to be conquered and carried to faraway places. But He brings some of them back to the Promised Land. The books of Esther (*You will love it*), Ezra & Nehemiah tell these stories (*some harsh realities to contend with*).

Now, God sends the People of Israel many prophets during all these days to warn them about the consequences of their sin. Some prophets wrote books containing their messages and predictions. These are found in Isaiah, Jeremiah, Lamentation, Ezekiel, Daniel, Hosea, Joel, Amos, Obadiah, Jonah, Micah, Nahum, Habakkuk, Zephaniah, Haggai, Zechariah, and Malachi. (*If you read that out loud, breathe will you?!*) Again, many of their predictions concern God's future salvation through David's son, and His judgment against sinful humanity. (*Powerful, but hard on occasion*)

In addition to these books, we have Psalms (*a favorite for many*) that records inspired worship and prayer. Many Psalms were written by Israel's great Prophet king, David.

Some books, like Job, Proverbs, Ecclesiastes, & Song of Solomon, are wisdom discussions that teach how to live well. (*Feel free to argue, you're supposed to wrestle, but in the end, God is right and you're wrong*)

Then we turn to the New Testament, where the promises of salvation are fulfilled in the coming of Jesus. The Gospels of Matthew, Mark, Luke, and John tell about Jesus' life, death, resurrection, and Church establishment. Luke goes on in Acts to tell the story of the early Church, focusing on specific men like Peter, Stephen, Philip, and Paul.

During those days, many issues forced Christian leaders to write letters. These letters, from Paul, Peter, James, John, and Jude[32] contain inspired messages to struggling people. (*Not hard, but you have to follow the flow of reason and argument.*)

Finally, we find the Book of Revelation (*Needs informed discussion*). It's written in a style called apocalyptic, which was common then, weird now. It uses symbols to preach powerful promises to a persecuted Church waiting for the return of Jesus Christ.

My advice? Read the Gospels and Acts. Read Psalms and wrestle through Proverbs. Make a plan to read cover to cover thereafter. Three chapters a day will finish the whole Bible in one year. If something puzzles you, or freaks you out, write down questions for your Bible believing pastor. And if he's not a Bible believing pastor, get another one who is.

~Andrew D. Sargent, Ph.D.

---

[32] Both James & Jude were Jesus' brothers who disbelieved until Jesus' resurrection.

# Reflections & Responses

When you get a chance, read The Book of Ruth... Naomi is really the central character. It is a perfect three act play (Chapter 1=Act 1, Chapter 2&3=Act 2 parts A&B, Chapter 4=Act 3) Write down some questions here about the story as you read. Then find someone who knows the Bible and ask them the questions you wrote down. Put their answers here too.

# DAY TEN
## Wrestle Scripture; Grow Strong

When I was working on my first Master's degree in Biblical Studies, a classmate and I were sitting in my living room, tussling over the meaning of a certain passage of Scripture. We were sharing life experiences, considering nerdy stuff like grammar, examining the context, and basically wrestling with the passage together in light of our varied lives and cultures. We were having a good time.

Then his wife chimed in rather haughtily, "You scholar types… always trying to figure out what a Bible passage means. I just read it and believe it." I hardly knew what to say. "I just read it, and believe it"?! What does that even mean?

My wife, Melodie, asked her, "How do you know what to believe if you haven't taken the time to even figure out what it's really saying?" I knew there was a reason I married her.

When you tell people that the Bible is God's Word, written by inspired prophets to teach the people of God about God, man, and reality, helping them to find the path of life and to avoid the path of death for this world and the next, some of them get the idea that wrestling with Scripture shows a lack of faith or even arrogance. But what if I told you that God expects you to wrestle faithfully with Scripture?[33] Would that surprise you? That, however, IS the way of wisdom.

I am fully invested in the inspiration of the Scriptures. My attitude toward them is "Let God be true and every man a liar." I trust the Bible more than I trust myself, more than I trust self-proclaimed and commonly recognized experts, more than I trust my mother and father. And let me tell you, that's a lot of trust. I believe that in every single place that Scripture and I are in conflict, it is Scripture that is right. So I must wrestle with it. Maybe I have misunderstood the text; maybe I have misunderstood the world, have a misconception about myself or others, but one way or another it is right and I am wrong.

Does that seem a contradiction? It's not. To say, "I just read it and believe it!" is not a statement of faith; it is a statement of arrogance; it is to say, I'm so smart and soooo wise that I know what Scripture means and obey it perfectly with just a casual glance. It confuses acceptance of the truth of a passage for the

---

[33] When I say, wrestle faithfully, I do not mean that one should be skeptical or cynical, only believing what the text says once he or she has ferreted out every detail, proven every angle beyond even a shadow of a doubt. I've had students who sided against Scripture and in favor of themselves and refused to budge unless I could eradicate any ability for them to even imagine a reason to doubt. This is NOT faithful wrestling.

meaty-muddy-gritty process of internalizing the message and making it your own in a deeply personal and practical way.

Me? I'm not smart enough and definitely not wise enough to fully digest the meaning of a passage of scripture with a light reading. I need to wrestle with it, and by doing so, make myself and my connection to its truths stronger.

I need first to make sure I understand what it is saying in its original context. I need to figure out what the author was attempting to accomplish in the lives of his original audience by what he said and in the way he said it. This is ancient literature, and though being ancient doesn't in any way diminish its vitality as divine word, it does form a gulf between it and myself. I need to enter the author's world and try my best to hear him correctly. Many Scriptures yield their secrets straightforwardly, but some will prove challenging, some will demand years of meditation and the right kind of human experiences to put me in the right frame to get it.

Next, I need to understand my own world and how the truths of the biblical writer might relate to modern struggles... and it does relate... far more than modern people tend to know. The hustle and bustle of modern technological life does not change human nature, so it does not change how Scripture relates to us. Rather, the whirl of modern life, its busyness, its noisiness, merely distracts us from asking important questions about our own existence, and keeps us striving to find truth in folly and meaning in purposelessness.

The paths of life and death have not readjusted themselves to accommodate electricity, motors, and the digital world. Thus, I wrestle with Scripture because it changes me in my willing defeat before it, and it strengthens me through the struggle. I make it my own so I can live it naturally and intuitively, rather than through some kind of "white-knuckle-ing" determination that I WILL walk the perfect line of divine command even though I have not allowed the Holy Spirit to change my inner-self as needed for faithful obedience.

What a torment it must be, for instance, to even imagine a life of monogamy and fidelity when one has never disciplined themselves in matters of sexual restraint and self-control. Such a one needs a radical change on the inside, a determination born of divine word, and the empowerment of God's Holy Spirit on the road. One's entire perception of reality needs alteration.

So, when Scripture calls us, for another instance, to a life of honesty and to a life of submission to authority, how does that relate to those who sought to save Jews from being murdered by the Nazis? How should we deal with democratic governments, where the rule of the people are the foundation of the society, or republics where a constitution is the law of the land? What should someone do when those in authority over them command wickedness or make righteousness illegal? What should we do about government corruption? Dishonest officials? Laws that violate the most basic principles of Scripture? How does one passage about honesty or submission to authority relate to the rest of Scripture? Does this one text or groups of texts stand in tension with others? Does this tension invalidate Scripture, or create a richness of wisdom in a complicated world full of human selfishness?

So, while part of me cries out before every passage of Scripture, "Let God be true, and every man a liar!" another part knows that I am weak in understanding and wisdom and weak in my resolve toward obedience. I study to improve my understanding, and wrestle with Scripture before a messy world in order to increase my wisdom. I cry out to God together with that overwhelmed father in Mark 9:24, "I believe, help my unbelief."

~Andrew D. Sargent, Ph.D.

# Reflections & Responses

The Bible is both deep and wide. It is a book that we could study day and night for a lifetime and still have treasures left untold. One thing I have learned as I have studied the Bible, is that the more I learn, the more I realize that I don't know. This is not a discouragement in any way – this is part of what makes the task of learning the Bible so enjoyable! The richness of God's revelation through Scripture is never ending and full of life. We will read and read the Bible and in turn it will read us.

As you begin to gather your questions, invite the Holy Spirit to illuminate passages for you to help you learn more about yourself, the world in which we live, and the ways that God relates to both. Find another friend or trusted Bible loving leader in your faith community that can sit with you and discuss the questions or even concerns you have about the Bible. Don't be surprised when you discover that the Bible is reflecting things back to you about yourself and how you relate to the world. This is part of the transforming power of God's Word.

As an exercise, Read Psalm 23. Write any questions that come to you as you read here. When you get a chance, asks someone who knows the Bible those questions. Then come back and pen in their answers.

# DAY ELEVEN
## Christians Seek a Church Family

Christians go to church. We practice our faith in community, as the Bible tells us to.[34] We are a global family of faith with local gatherings almost everywhere—"Churches."

"Church" is used to translate the Greek, *Ekklēsia,* which is a combination of "call" and "out." So many quip, we're *called out ones...* which is fun and makes us feel special... but it is also misleading. *Ekklēsia* is used to speak of any public assembly whether political, religious, or even a neighborhood block party. The English word *church*, however, isn't directly connected to *Ekklesia* at all, being in point of fact, a word connected to the Greek *kuriakon* for "belonging to the Lord," who is *kurios*.[35]

In modern days, one group of believers gather on the North side of Main Street and another group on the south side, one mile from yet another set at the corner of Watts and Happening. One group calls themselves Baptists, another Pentecostal, or Lutheran, or Episcopalian, Methodist, Catholic, or Something-Orthodox. Some, usually without higher association, might even call themselves things like, *First Church of the Last Chance World on Fire Revival*, or *Hell is Licking at Your Heels Assembly,* or *His Church.*

Now know... yes, I'm serious... that this reality is not as ominous as it sounds. There is a reasonable history behind this multiplicity, and a healthy pattern of revitalization in the continued expansion, which I will discuss in another devotional.

For now, let me merely explain the intended nature of church as revealed in both its establishment on the day of Pentecost in Acts 2, and throughout the rest of the New Testament.

Believe it or not, the story of the birth of THE Church in Acts 2 is written to meet the sorrows and hopes of a prophecy in Isaiah 59. Isaiah 59 begins by bemoaning the depth and darkness of human evil in the world. In verse 16, it turns to God's reaction. Knowing that help and hope is beyond man in themselves, He, poetically, determines to bring salvation Himself. In verse 20, this help is God coming to Jerusalem in a glorious manifestation of Holy Spirit power through the work of a divine redeemer who will make a covenant with the faithful and seal this covenant through the giving of His Holy Spirit... like a

---

[34] Hebrews 10:25 in the New Testament says, *"And let us not neglect our meeting together, as some people do, but encourage one another, especially now that the day of his return is drawing near."*

[35] My Greek reading friends are slapping their knees in laughter over that last bit. *Kurios* means Lord... but also looks like curious... so... well... never mind, sorry I brought it up.

wedding of sorts. These shall become a multigenerational community of Spirit-filled believers speaking His Word to the world.

In Acts 2, God's Holy Spirit breaks into the ugliness of human history in the wake of Jewish and Roman cooperative evil in the murder of Jesus, humanity's only innocent man. Upon His resurrection, Jesus commands His followers to make disciples from all the nations of the earth and promises that His Holy Spirit will come to lead and empower them in that work. He does, He did, He is.

In the story, we have the explosive arrival of the Spirit in displays of power and wonders. Once-terrified Peter marches boldly before the Jews gathered in Jerusalem from every place they'd scattered over the centuries; he shuts down hecklers, explains the gospel, opens the Scriptures powerfully for their understanding, establishes the deity of Jesus, confronts their guilt and sin, and calls for their repentance. The reaction is overwhelming and the Disciples-turned-Apostles incorporate thousands of new believers into an instantly formed body called The Church.

In the last part, of Acts 2, though often treated like a closing epilogue, a cute wrap up, we find the ultimate answer to Isaiah's hopes and humanity's need. All that power and wonder, preaching and conviction, repentance and commitment find their crescendo, their purposed end, in the planting of a community of super-natural love. Here a citizen of a debase and lost world can, through the power of the Holy Spirit, escape his or her own selfishness and the misery it produces and find true community. Believers dedicate themselves to the biblical teaching of Jesus' disciples, to prayer, to sharing their meals together, joyously sacrificing to meet the emergency needs of those who stay in Jerusalem rather than returning to their homes in foreign parts. The world had never seen anything like it. The world was never able to produce anything akin… neither Jew nor Gentile… in the history of man.

It is not surprising then, that the Apostle Paul, throughout his writings, routinely speaks of being Christian as joining a covenant community even tighter than family. Hence the old saw, "The blood of the covenant is thicker than the water of the womb."[36] What did you think "Blood is thicker than water" meant? One God the Father, One Jesus, One Holy Spirit, one faith, one body of Christ.[37]

I have met believers in over ten countries and the bond that I have felt with them was instant and strong. They are my brothers and sisters in the Lord. I once watched intrigued as a Hindu shop owner berated an Indian Christian for protecting me and my traveling companion from his malicious designs. As it was translated to me, he yelled, "We two are Indians, we should both take these white men's money!" That Indian Christian, who had known me mere days, told him, "They are my brothers, and I will not allow you to steal from them."

---

[36] In modern times we've flipped this on its head, taking blood as family bond, and water as… well… as water I guess.

[37] 1 Corinthians 8:6; 10:17; 12:1-13:13.

If this was true in its founding, and is true now even across nations, how much more should it be reflected in our local congregations. The Church community should be like family, and family works through problems. If I gave you a list of all the things my siblings have done to me over the years, you'd wonder why I still speak to them… but speak to them I do… all the time… getting together as often as we can. We are family… we have worked and continue to work through our issues. We are one. This should be our Christian commitment to oneness.

Pray, therefore, "Lord, you want your people to be one. Help me find a church that shares my commitments to You, to Your Word, to Your Mission, and to Your call for us to be one. Help me find a church family."

~Andrew D. Sargent, Ph.D.

# Reflections & Responses

If you have not already found a church community to belong to, begin the search today. As you are considering which church, review the last full paragraph of Day 12 when you get there and use it as a checklist. Sincerely look for the qualities of a Bible believing community of believers. Commit to attend a church that believes in the whole Bible and preaches God's word first and foremost. Listing some of the churches around you. Visit their websites and take some notes here on your impression of them.

If you are in a church but haven't connected with anyone yet, reach out to volunteer or serve somewhere in the church, ask about a small group where you might connect with other believers. Whatever your next step to building community within your church is, make the commitment to take that next step this week. If you have found a good church but have only gone to church occasionally, commit to going weekly, and pick an extra event to attend where you can start building a closer relationship with others in the church. Gathering together regularly isn't just a good idea, it is God's ideal for us as believers. List some of the things going on in the church you are attending that might offer you an opportunity to serve and/or build some closer relationship there.

# DAY TWELVE
## Don't Shop or Hop… Find a Church Family

There is an old joke that goes, "If I found the perfect Church, it wouldn't be once I joined." And that is as good of an anchor to toss out as any other when discussing the right and wrong way to choose a church family.

In the early days, after the Day of Pentecost,[38] there was no choice. There was one Church (Capital C) overseen by both the disciples and the brothers of Jesus, all turned "Apostles." As the gospel spread the one Church still had only one church (small c) per community. This one Church—called "Catholic," meaning *universal*[39]—had many house meetings, but only one authority structure. If someone stole your favorite seat by the window, you could get angry, but hopping to another house meeting was highly impractical, and would hardly be tolerated. Like with family, if you were a believer, you were pretty much stuck having to work it out; there was nowhere else to go… and Christians go to church.

The present state of things with multiple church organizations boasting varied-but-similar beliefs and practices, sometimes next door to each other, has its origin in two historical realities: Administrative demands & The slippery slope toward organizational death.

Some churches yield over generations to the natural lean of the human heart toward self-gratification in greed, pride, lust, envy, wrath, sloth and gluttony. Excitement wanes; beliefs become customs; passion for Scripture cools; generations slowly conform themselves to the world around them.

Some find revitalization from this death spiral from within. Others don't… forcing true disciples of Jesus to start something new elsewhere in order to worship truly, freely, and honestly.

In the 1500s, when the "Catholic" authority structures refused to be revitalized, many reformers risked their lives to break free, and new churches sprang up around the world. They began independent from each other by administrative necessity and spread. Lutherans spread from Germany, Anglicans from England, Presbyterians from Scotland, etc. These were called protest churches… i.e. Protestant Churches.

These Protestant Churches, born from spiritual revitalization, succumbed over time to the impatience of frustrated reformers more easily than did the One Universal Catholic Church. Influential leaders with particular thoughts about faith and practice broke free more handily to start their own fellowships with

---

[38] You can read the story of the Church's beginning in Acts 1-2 in the New Testament.

[39] The term "*katholikos*" was first used to describe the Church in A.D. 107 by Ignatius of Antioch.

less consequence than of old. Breaking free to revitalize became part of the pattern.

So now, we have First Baptist across the street from 4th Baptist which is a quarter mile from 2nd Presbyterian, which is next to Saint Theresa's, just a wee bit down the road in one direction from New Hope Assembly of God, and in the other from that independent place called, Corner Stone. They don't necessarily hate each other, though Lucy Maude Montgomery books[40] are filled with humorous tales of the once upon a time antagonism between the Presbyterians, Baptists, and Methodists on Prince Edward Island. In fact, their leaders might even belong to the same pastors' fellowship group and plan mutual events like concerts or fund raisers for charity. But they are not the same, not exactly. They differ in their tradition, history, and values, their religious habits, perceptions of worship, church administration, the role of the Church in life and society, and, to some extent, about biblical interpretation and theological issues big and small.

So who's got it right?

Me, of course. I would have thought that was obvious to you by now.

But on a more serious note, how can you decide where to plant yourself in terms of joining a church? And when I say "plant yourself" I mean it. Find a church family and be a part of what is going on there. Be present. Give financially through both tithes and special offerings. Get involved in the work of the ministry of that church… and I don't just mean doing nursery once a month.

Now, the benefit of modern church diversity is the pressure it puts on congregations to keep faith fresh and mission passionate.

It can also, however, facilitate a kind of consumerism regarding church "attendance." Your kid doesn't get the lead in the passion play? "Well, we'll just go on over to Life church, I'm sure they'd be glad to have the talents of my precious angel at their disposal, stuttering and all." Think your church asks for money too much? "Let's start going over to Our Lady of Perpetual Poverty, they obviously won't be hitting us up so often!" You walk in the door of a new church and test the sanctuary seating for comfort, the lobby for ambiance, and check out the list of programs for the kiddos.

I get it. Some churches have Sanford-and-Son property and Welcome-Back-Kotter Youth programs. They minister to the lowest and most difficult communities. And what sensible set of parents trying to raise good Christian kids want those kinds of influences in their life. Right?! That, of course, is a consumer's perspective, asking what one can get from a congregation, rather than what one can learn, or how faith and obedience can grow, or how one can help in the work of advancing the Kingdom of God in the hearts of lost souls here vs. there.

---

[40] She wrote the Anne of Green Gables series and many other novels and short stories set on Prince Edward Island.

You need to be where God wants you, which requires prayerful listening... but it also requires honest assessments, not of the freebies, but of the message and mission of a church, the earnestness of the leadership, the strength of the word preached. We should find a place that preaches the Scriptures properly and trains people how to read it better... one that takes theology seriously, preaches on sin and your transformation into the image of Jesus. It should be concerned with spreading the gospel, discipling believers new and old, supporting missions and missionaries. It should take the worship experience seriously and both practice and promote prayer and sensitivity to the Holy Spirit. Leadership should be accountable to some higher authority, and to some extent to the congregation, to faith statements firmly rooted in Scripture, and ultimately and truly to Scripture itself.

If you can find this, adopt the whole lot of them into your family circle, pray for them every day, and thank God that they are in your life... even when they tick you off.

~Andrew D. Sargent, Ph.D.

# Reflections & Responses

Take each of the categories of concerns in the second to the last paragraph above and write them here as a kind of check list. If you are looking for a church, bring this list along with you when you go to service. In a non-judgmental way make notes here about how the church you visit this week measures up. You may have to ask some people who attend that church how they think they measure up to the list. Make it informative and fun, not anxiety ridden or hostile.

# DAY THIRTEEN
## Weird Things Like Baptism & Communion

If you are a new believer, fresh to the church scene, Christians can, I imagine, seem like really nice people who do some weird things. One of the reasons that they do some weird things is because they continue religious practices from the Bible. The old stuff is 4000 years old, but on the plus side, the new stuff is only 2000 years old… barely out of diapers. When only decades old Christians engage in ancient rituals and use old-timey phrases from a Bible translated in 1611, it must appear as odd as if they came to church in Bedouin robes and a giant turban, looking for a place to tie up their camel. Tip: They like the shady spot next to the water trough. I looked it up.

So, today, I want to introduce you to a single subject from the ancient world—Covenant—that effects two weird things in church: Baptism and Communion.

Put simply, covenant is like a contract that is enforced by spiritual agents. So, a pagan who believes in, say, Marduk (*The ancient storm god, not that mischievous but hilarious great Dane*) may not be trusted by the guy who rents out camels, but when that same guy swears to bring it back without a mark on it and calls upon Marduk to have ravens pick out his eyes if he doesn't, we are getting at the soul of covenant.

When a person makes a covenant, they make promises to engage or refrain from certain activities and seal that promise with self-cursing oaths before God/gods whom the parties believe in… thus they believe that He/they really will punish them if they prove unfaithful.[41]

There are hundreds of covenants in Scripture. In fact, just eating a meal together was a covenant-making act. It was a special kind of evil to seek the harm of someone with whom you've "broken bread." Even so, there are only a handful of really big covenants, ones that involve nations and generations. They have different forms depending on the parties and the promises. I certainly can't cover them all here, but the idea is important to grasp.

Covenants in Scripture tend to have ritual acts that start a covenant; it's like signing a contract. Now, however unsettling it may feel to modern folks, these ritual acts usually symbolize the self-cursing/death of those making them. Eating a meal together symbolized ingesting divine curses. Do you feel all devotionally yet? We'll get there… I hope.

In the ancient world, men stood before gods and governments on behalf of their families. So, when God makes a covenant with Abraham "and his seed" this covenant is entered into symbolically with the circumcision of the males,

---

[41] By the way, marriage is a covenant of lifelong sexual exclusivity in the building of family.

who are each to become heads of their own households. It shed blood (*but healed without real harm*) and symbolized the cutting off of "posterity" (*Future generations*). It was a first act and a lifelong reminder of one's covenant with the Creator.

In the decades before Jesus' birth, groups of Jews started special assemblies and made special religious commitments beyond being Jewish. So, naturally, they began to seek out initiation rites they could use. Not only was circumcision already taken, but they also wanted something that could be performed by women as well.[42] They chose a modest ritual bath. It was priestly, because priests washed before entering holy places. It also symbolized washing away the past, and was a popular image for death and resurrection as well. Oh yeah, and it symbolized Moses bringing Israel to a new life through the Red Sea, and Joshua to a new life through the Jordan River. It was perfect.

It was sooooo perfect, that Jesus used it with those who joined His spiritual family in what the ancient prophets called "The New Covenant." After Jesus' death and resurrection, baptism took on even more symbolism. In baptism, we each symbolically memorialize Jesus' death and resurrection and publicly declare our promise to fulfill all the responsibilities involved in joining Jesus' "Church."

Another element of covenants, was that people had signs that they were in a covenant. These worked as reminders of their responsibilities and promises and as a witness to others. We do this, when we wear wedding rings. Israelites wore tassels on their outer garments. Sometimes these signs were also ritual acts, like eating a sacred meal together with layers of symbolism, one of which was always invoking curses as an oath. The Israelites celebrated Passover for instance, and Jesus, as with baptism, added special symbolism to the Passover meal to represent memorializing the New Covenant which was sealed with Jesus' death and validated in His resurrection.

It was common in the early Church, after their service of prayer, worship, and preaching, to eat a community meal together. It replaced the Passover supper in time as "The Lord's Supper." They called these meals, "love feasts," which had ZERO sexual undertones, but sure did cause some rumors among the Romans.

Now, if you were a Roman soldier, you routinely took a loyalty oath to Caesar. You renewed your promises to serve or die by his command by taking bread and wine from "Caesar's table." It's not the same thing as eating a Caesar's Salad, don't worry.

So, as time passed, and as the Church became more and more non-Jewish, this taking of bread and wine replaced the love feast that replaced Passover as "The Lord's Supper." Many churches call this sacred "meal" Communion. When you take it, you are supposed to consider the layers of its meaning and your covenant with Jesus… part of which is living in harmony with fellow

---

[42] Female "circumcision" is NOT the same as male circumcision… it does permanent harm. The very idea of it was despised and rejected by Jewish worshippers.

believers. So, as you eat the bread and drink the cup, examine yourself and ask, "How am I doing with the Lord?" and "How am I doing with the Lord's people?"

When you are baptized and take communion in church, you are continuing a covenant tradition that connects you to believers as far back as Abraham & Sarah who broke bread with the angel of the Lord and made a covenant with their Creator.[43] It maybe feels a little weird at first, but it is also, super cool.

~ Andrew D. Sargent, Ph.D.

---

[43] Genesis 12, 15, 17 & 18. The first book in the Bible.

# Reflections & Responses

Discuss a few ways that learning about "covenant" might help you better understand baptism and communion?

If you haven't been baptized, prayerfully consider taking this next step in your faith journey. Describe your past understanding of baptism and how this new information impacts your thinking on it.

As you come to communion going forward, earnestly ask the Lord about the health of your relationship with Him. Earnestly pray about the health of your relationships with other believers as well. Take a moment to listen to the Holy Spirit, confess anything that needs to be confessed, and if necessary, make amends with a brother or sister in Christ. These are all steps of our covenant of communion. Here, however, describe your past understanding of communion and how this new information impacts your thinking on it.

# DAY FOURTEEN
## Cultivating Mindfulness of Christian Virtues

The big ideas about life need to be woven into the daily, weekly, monthly and yearly routines of living if one wants to keep important Christian virtues fresh… like gratitude, repentance, mercy, and forgiveness. The perpetual rehearsal of core values in the seemingly mundane aspects of life as well as in special periods of remembrance and holiday keep one mindful of them, shaping choices and attitudes alike every day.

Do you want your children to reap the benefits of a disciplined life? Then train them to order their world when it is small. Keep your room neat. Take care of your toys. Wait your turn without complaining. Make your bed. Dress nice for special occasions. Church is a special occasion. Eat as a family at mealtime… and set the table. Focus on hygiene. Brush and floss teeth. Go to bed clean. Get clean after dirty or sweaty work. Keep clothes and hair tidy. Orderly habits keep one mindful of an ordered life.

Do you want respectful and grateful kids? Train them to say, "Please," "Thank you," "Yes, Sir," "No, Ma'am." Teach them to help the weak and to hold doors for people behind them. That alone trains them to be mindful of the impact their actions have on others in every situation not just when exiting or entering buildings.

Jewish worshippers memorialize important events from their history and fill their celebrations with symbols that preach important things about these events. Rosh Hashanah (*New Year*) proves an intuitive time for reflection on gratitude for counted blessings, repentance for remembered failures, and resolutions to do better. Yom Kippur (*Day of Atonement*) is a day of fasting, mourning, and repentance for sin. It rejoices in the mercy of God's forgiveness. Passover celebrates deliverance from Egyptian bondage… a longstanding image for deliverance from a slavery to sin and the provision for salvation in the Passover Lamb. Shavuot (*Pentecost*) has more layers than a prize wedding cake with celebrations ranging from harvests to the birth and death of King David, and the giving of the Law through Moses.

Every week, they keep Sabbath (*Friday sunset to Saturday sunset*), dedicating a day to Spiritual remembrance, a day of "being" not "doing," rest for themselves and rest for those serving them. It cultivates mindfulness about the value of people over production and the joy of just existing at peace in God's world, however much man has made a mess of it. It is family stopping together to just enjoy each other's presence before God their Creator. Here, each year, they also cycle through the entire Tanakh together (*Old Testament*).

Christians celebrate Sundays as a similar day to Sabbath. We have largely lost the full Jewish mindfulness of a day of rest, living now in a 24/7 culture, but Church is traditionally held on this day to commemorate the resurrection of Jesus on the morning of the third day—*Crucified on Friday and resurrected on Sunday*. We are called to pray "without ceasing," suggesting a life of mindfulness about God and communication with Him, but on Sundays, our services are dedicated to prayer, as well as to giving, and worship, fellowship (*meaning hanging with fellow Christians*) and being instructed from the Scriptures in the path of life and the way of Christian service.

Christians celebrate holidays like Thanks Giving, New Years, Valentine's Day, Mother's and Father's Days and use each to promote mindfulness of particular Christian virtues, like gratitude. We also have three major Christian celebrations: Resurrection Sunday (*Often called Easter*), Pentecost Sunday, and Christmas.

"Easter" has many elements of the celebration of newness of life, Spring as some type of resurrection... hence the chicks and bunnies and colored eggs in baskets lined with fake grass... and who doesn't love a peep or chocolate rabbit now and then... Cadbury! Take me away!!!!! BUT Resurrection Sunday, preceded with several days of special memorializing of the "passion week"[44] is about Jesus' death and resurrection to the glorified life promised someday to ALL who believe. Death and resurrection proved His claims of deity and to being Israel's Christ/Messiah. It was the validation of all the promises of God in the Old Testament including the promise of eternal life with God. Here is mindfulness of sin, repentance, and divine mercy through the willing self-sacrifice of Jesus; thus, gratitude, purpose, and mission.

The next, great Christian holiday, one unfortunately ignored by many denominations, is Pentecost Sunday, which occurs on the 7th Sunday after Easter, which occurs on the first Sunday after the first full moon after Spring Equinox on September 21st. Now, isn't that fun? I think it's fun. Just another joyous converging of lunar (*moon*) calendars and solar (*sun*) calendars. Here, when Jews are doing their own magnificent and layered celebrations, Christians are celebrating the coming of the Holy Spirit, sent by Christ to those putting their faith in Him.[45] Here, we cultivate mindfulness of our ongoing dependence on the Spirit of God to become more and more like Jesus, to do the work that God has called us to do, to be a people shining God's power and light into human darkness.

Jesus was not born on December 25th, but for noble purposes, not evil purposes as many have been told, Church leaders chose this date to celebrate the incarnation of God in the coming of Jesus. As you may notice, advent calendars celebrate for a whole month leading up to the day. Many of our traditions associated with Christmas emphasize Christian values, like giving gifts, kindness, and a spirit of generosity, special care for the poor, feasting on the bounty of God's provision in recent harvests, and coming together with

---

[44] Important stuff that happened the week they crucified Jesus, like Jesus' triumphal ride into Jerusalem, his trial on Thursday night, and his crucifixion on Friday.
[45] Read Acts chapter 2 in the New Testament.

friends and family to love and appreciate one another. There is beauty and decoration… dazzling lights in darkening days, and joy, and treats. We have many songs written for the occasion and sing them EVERYWHERE beginning the day after Thanks Giving on to New Years. Perhaps your Christmas celebrations looked a little different, but this is the mindfulness to cultivate in future celebrations.

Holidays and patterns done well, cultivate a life changing mindfulness of great Christian virtues.

~Andrew D. Sargent, Ph.D.

# Reflections & Responses

Describe some of your favorite holiday memories?

Enjoyed or annoyed, jot down a few special traditions your family had for any holidays?

In what ways does your faith in Jesus inspire you to bring new meaning to holidays and traditions in your life?

List a few ways in which you might mindfully celebrate the Lord throughout your week?

Consider taking time to "sabbath," take a rest day, or a day of gratitude and being with your family or your family of believers. If you get the chance to do this, consider coming back here to note of anything God impresses upon you as you express gratefulness for His provision and rest in His presence.

# DAY FIFTEEN
## Weird Thoughts about the Holy Spirit

**A Tip for Reading: You may want to read through at first just taking it all in, without looking everything up. Then it would be beneficial to you to take time later to look up each reference as you read through again... for there are many.**

I noted earlier that a lot of the weird things that modern Christians do are weird because they are anything but modern. They are, rather, modern attempts to practice ancient things like covenant through things like communion, and baptism.

Another weird thing that modern Christians talk about... a lot... is the Holy Spirit. God is spirit, so the idea of the Holy Spirit is not much of a mental stretch. What's weird is the WAY Christians speak of the Holy Spirit, claiming that they are "filled"[46] with the Holy Spirit, that they have the "gift"[47] of the Holy Spirit that "falls"[48] "leads,"[49] "speaks,"[50] "is poured out,"[51] and pours out.[52] We speak of the Holy Spirit changing us in "regeneration"[53] and "indwelling"[54] us and "convicting"[55] us, "guiding"[56] us, "sanctifying"[57] us.

One of the things that adds to the oddity of Holy Spirit talk is what many perceive to be a late introduction of the idea that born again believers[58] would someday "receive"[59] the Holy Spirit, be "baptized"[60] in the Holy Spirit, and under this new condition operate in supernatural gifts of the Holy Spirit.[61]

---

[46] Luke 1:41, 67; Acts 2:4, 4:8, 31, 9:17, 13:9, 52; Ephesians 5:18
[47] Acts 1:45, 2:38, 10:45, 11:17; Hebrews 6:4, also called the promise of the Holy Spirit Luke 24:49, Acts 1:4, 2:33, 39, 7:17.
[48] Acts 10:44, 11:15.
[49] Matthew 4:1; Luke 4:1; John Romans 8:14; Galatians 5:18.
[50] Acts 4:31; 1 Corinthians 14:2; Ephesians 1:13, 6:17.
[51] Acts 2:17-18, 10:45; Romans 5:5.
[52] Acts 2:33.
[53] Titus 3:5.
[54] John 14:17; Romans 8:9, 11; 1 Corinthians 3:16; 2 Timothy 1:14; James 4:5.
[55] John 16:7-11; Acts 2:37.
[56] John 16:7-15
[57] John 17:17-19; Acts 20:32, 26:18; Romans 6:19-22, 15:16; 1 Corinthians 1:2, 30, 6:11; Ephesians 5:26; 1 Thessalonians 4:3, 5:23; 2 Thessalonians 2:13; Hebrews 2:11, 9:13, 10:10-29; 1 Peter 1:2.
[58] John 1:33, 3:5-34,
[59] John 7:39, 14:17, 20:22; Acts 2:33-38, 8:15-19, 10:47, 19:2; Romans 8:15; 1 Corinthians 2:12; Galatians 3:2, 14.
[60] Matthew 3:11; Mark 1:8; Luke 3:16; John 1:33; Acts 1:5, 11:16; 1 Corinthians 12:13.
[61] Acts 1:8; 1 Corinthians 12-14; Ephesians 4:8-16; 1 Timothy 4:14; Hebrews 2:4; James 1:17; 1 Peter 4:7-11

I cannot deal with the entirety of what is called Pneumatology (study of the Holy Spirit), whose details can cause not a little contention even among devout Bible-believing Christians, but I do want to put these issues on your radar. I will add, however, that if you know *nothing* of such encounters with the Holy Spirit, that lack might be a check-engine light blinking in your soul. Whatever label you may give it (I prefer biblical labels) cry out to God that you might walk in the fullness of His Holy Spirit as manifested in the pages of the New Testament.[62]

Contrary to what many imagine the promise of the Holy Spirit is not new in the New Testament. It is not new to the prophetic writers like Isaiah,[63] Ezekiel,[64] and Joel,[65] who predicted that all the faithful of the Lord would someday be filled with the Holy Spirit, letting God speak the divine word through them and manifesting power from on high through Spiritual gifts. The promise of the Holy Spirit is not new to the early kings who received a taste of this promise in the empowerment to lead, like Saul[66] who had the Holy Spirit taken from him, and David who feared that the same might happen to him because of a terrible series of sins committed in a dark period in his life.[67] Indeed, it is not new to the Judges of Israel,[68] nor to Moses the great prophet who did mighty deeds through the empowerment of God,[69] nor even to the ancient fathers like Abraham, Isaac, Jacob and Joseph who met with the Lord and saw the Spirit of God do wonders.[70]

The first promise of the Holy Spirit is given without those express words in the very creation of man.

While many debate what it means to be "made in the image of God," what's called "the *Imago Dei*," the essential meaning of that making is in the nature of the word "image" which is one of two main words used concerning the idols of pagans, as in Numbers 33:52, *"Then ye shall drive out all the inhabitants of the land from before you, and destroy all their pictures, and destroy all their molten images,"* and 2 Kings 11:18, *"Then all the people of the land went to the house of Baal and tore it down; his altars and his images they broke in pieces."*

The pagans didn't worship wood and stone and metal, they worshipped carvings that through magic rituals they made into spiritual portals for the god

---

[62] Remember though, things recorded in Scripture are extraordinary moments in lives that looked very much like yours and mine. We shouldn't compare our daily grind to someone else's highlight reel. I've had extraordinary moments in the Lord, led on by the Holy Spirit, as have many of the other believers I know, but mostly, life is… just life.

[63] Isaiah 11:2, 32:15, 37:7, 42:1, 44:3, 59:21, 61:1, 63:14

[64] Ezekiel 2:2, 3:12-24, 11:5, 36:26-27, 37:1-14, 39:29.

[65] Joel 2:28-29

[66] I Samuel 10:10, 11:6, 16:14-23

[67] I Samuel 16:13; 2 Samuel 23:2; Psalm 51:11

[68] Judges 3:10, 6:34, 11:29, 13:25, 14:6, 19, 15:14.

[69] Exodus 35:31; Numbers 11:17-26; pay attention to the Mosaic hope in Numbers 11:29. Numbers 24:2 and 27:18

[70] Genesis 12:7, 17:1, 18:1, 26:2, 26:24, 20:2-8, 28:10-19, 31:8-13, 32:24-30, 41:38.

or goddess of any given temple so that said deity could rule and reign there. It was called, "opening the mouth"[71] of the idol.

Both Genesis creation stories use Temple imagery. In Genesis 2, God establishes the garden of Eden as a garden Temple and sets in it His living Image/Idol to rule and reign on His behalf just as He declares of their making in Genesis 1:26-28:

*"Then God said: Let us make man in our image, after our*
*likeness. And let them have dominion over the fish of the sea*
*and over the birds of the heavens and over the livestock and*
*over all the earth and over every creeping thing that creeps on*
*the earth. So God created man in his own image, in the image*
*of God he created him; male and female he created them. And*
*God blessed them. And God said to them, "Be fruitful and*
*multiply and fill the earth and subdue it, and have dominion*
*over the fish of the sea and over the birds of the heavens and*
*over every living thing that moves on the earth."*

God likes to work cooperatively with His creatures and the highest of these on earth are those made to be His living image there, filled with His Holy Spirit, led by His Holy Spirit, instruments of His Holy Spirit, His representatives in the world… His regents.

We rebelled, however, and have continued to rebel against Him, against His mission, against His right of place in our lives. Thus, Adam became the father of a fallen race of selfish rebels. But even in that moment the promise of restoration came. In Genesis 3:16 God says to the serpent, *"I will put enmity between you and the woman, and between your offspring and her offspring; he shall bruise your head, and you shall bruise his heel."* This is the first promise of the coming of a Messiah who, it is revealed more fully in time, would repair the path between God and Man,[72] die a sacrificial death for all who will believe,[73] and resurrect to become a new father of a new race of men and women ready to fulfill their original purpose as God's Image bearers. And that is what begins anew in Acts chapter 2 in the coming of the Holy Spirit to fall, pour out, fill up, lead, empower, gift, and sanctify.

~Andrew D. Sargent, Ph.D.

---

[71] This is an important association in Isaiah's call into prophetic ministry in Isaiah 6.
[72] Ephesians 2:14-16
[73] Isaiah 52:12-53:12

# Reflections & Responses

When time permits, slowly reread this chapter with your Bible open. Look up the scripture references and read them alongside the chapter. Give yourself time to read and connect the Scriptures. Ask the Lord to help you have a better understanding of His Holy Spirit. Tip: A Bible App on your phone or laptop may allow you to look these up quickly. Write down anything in this process that strikes you as important. Write down areas of confusion or questions that arise. When bring these questions to a trusted friend or mentor in your faith community (church) come back here and write the answers to those questions.

# DAY SIXTEEN
## Can I Get a Witness?
## The Call to Be Salt & Light in a Dark and Rotten World

As a teenager I worked in a grocery store doing anything that needed doing, whether bagging, cashiering, stocking produce, or even painting the kick spaces on the shelves. How many times a day did customers say, "Laying down on the job, Aye!" while I was painting those spaces? Many, indeed. I laughed each time to please them.

One day, my job was to hang sales announcements in the front windows. As I got the first one up I noticed that it read "On SALE! Porterhorse Steaks 98¢ a pound." My boss told me to leave it. He wanted to see how many people noticed, and, perhaps, how many were disappointed to discover it was just regular beef.

It reminds me of those memes on social media that capture the results of a poorly done job... so poorly done that one is forced to stop in awe that someone walked away from it saying, "That should take care of that." One had a birthday cake that read "Happy Birthday, Jimmy in Italics." One has a street line painter who painted the lines out around a branch on the road. Another left a kid's bouncy house slide set to launch kids from above into a recessed highway backing the property. The caption for these usually runs, "You had one job to do."

We all know that life is filled with jobs to do and few have only one, but we also know that some responsibilities stand tall as supreme commission in the taking of a job. This includes being a Christian.

In Genesis man was made in God's image. While many debate all the implications of this origin, one things stands supreme... it is a commission to be filled with the Spirit of God and to work in this world as His regent... i.e. kings accountable to a higher king.

Man falls through rebellion, but is renewed to this call in the coming of the Holy Spirit in Acts 2. Jesus anticipates this renewal numerous times in the Gospels and announces in Acts 1:8 where, "But you will receive power when the Holy Spirit has come upon you, and you will be my witnesses in Jerusalem and in all Judea and Samaria, and to the end of the earth."

In this role, Jesus calls us Salt and Light... preservers and illumined guides to that which is rotting and lost in the darkness of both the human heart and the corrupt societies that human hearts build together. Matthew 5:13-16, declares, "You are the salt of the earth, but if salt has lost its taste, how shall its saltiness be restored? It is no longer good for anything except to be thrown out and trampled under people's feet. You are the light of the world. A city set on a hill cannot be hidden. Nor do people light a lamp and put it under a basket, but on a stand, and it gives light to all in the house. In the same way, let your light shine before others, so that they may see your good works and give glory to your Father who is in heaven."

The work of the Church is manifold. There are many jobs to do in teaching, preaching, evangelism, administration, discipline, training leaders, and building up the faithful to do the work of the ministry. We are each called to care for family, raise children in the Lord, cultivate strong marriages, to moral restraint, ethical living, and helping the less fortunate. We are called to spiritual disciplines like prayer, fasting, Christlikeness, worship, Bible Study. We are all called, in one way or another, to fulfill the purposes of Christ in us so that He can do the work of the Divine Kingdom through us.

Even so, one job stands tall among all the things we are called to as Believers—we are called to be witnesses. Jesus recognizes the centrality of this "you will be my witnesses" mission without dismissing the diverse work of Church and discipleship in Matthew 28:18-20, saying, "All authority in heaven and on earth has been given to me. Go therefore and make disciples of all nations, baptizing them in the name of the Father and of the Son and of the Holy Spirit, teaching them to observe all that I have commanded you."

There is a popular but anonymous saying often accredited to St. Francis of Assisi that goes, "Preach the gospel at all times and if necessary, use words." It highlights the need for our lives to back up our words… which St. Francis did say… "No brother should preach contrary to the form and regulations of the holy Church… All the Friars … should preach by their deeds." But this poignant statement is often wrongly used to suggest that a good life without preaching is preferred to actual preaching. Both Assisi and Paul would disagree.

In fact, Paul says in Romans 10:13-15"everyone who calls on the name of the Lord will be saved." Rom 10:14 "How then will they call on him in whom they have not believed? And how are they to believe in him of whom they have never heard? And how are they to hear without someone preaching? And how are they to preach unless they are sent? As it is written, "How beautiful are the feet of those who preach the good news!"

It may take time to find your voice, and your style and your particular area of strength, but whether by hook or by crook you have been called to be salt and light in a rotting and dark world. You have been called to witness for Christ. Pray therefore that Christ may guide you on your way, and be bold.

~Andrew D. Sargent, Ph.D.

# Reflections & Responses

Discuss how you first heard about Jesus? Where did you first hear about the good news of the saving grace of Jesus? Was it a friend? Did someone invite you to church? Did someone send you a reel about the saving power of Jesus?

Chances are, someone somewhere shared Jesus with you, or told you about some way that God was making a difference in their life that made you want to know more. This is what witnessing can look like. Yes, some are called to be pastors and preach from a pulpit, but we are all called to tell others about the good that God is working in our lives. That transformative power of the cross and resurrection that has changed your life is the very same thing that every other person around you needs to hear.

Have you told anyone about your experience with Jesus Christ? Write about that event here.

With this devotional in mind, take a chance this week and share what God has done in your life with someone… a friend… stranger… a coworker. Come back and write about it here.

# DAY SEVENTEEN
## The Greatest Commandment

Because the Creator is a God of love who, for His own purposes, made a good world for us to populate and to bring into divine order,[74] He is also eager to reveal Himself to us and to help us find the path of life in His world... no matter how badly we've messed it up.[75]

Therefore, in the Book of Exodus chapter 20, in the Old Testament, after He brought Israel out of forced labor in Egypt, God gives ten commandments to the Children of Abraham to help them find that path of life as a new nation. If any people, in any place, and any age, were to live by these commands, they would create a society of what the Bible calls "*SHALOM*" and "*ESHER*."[76] *SHALOM*, often translated as "peace," is a comprehensive vision for the good life of stability, wisdom, happiness, and wholeness... not a perfect society, because people still battle selfishness, but a blessed one... "*ESHER*."

Exodus 20:1-3 begins the ten saying, "*Then God spoke all these words, saying, 'I am the LORD[77] your God, who brought you out of the land of Egypt, out of the house of slavery. You shall have no other gods before Me.*" This first command lays the foundation for all the rest. Anyone who lives by these commands will be blessed by them. But, it is the Creator's world, and only those who wake up to Him and commit their way to Him can hope to find the truest riches of His path of life.

Pagan worshippers intuited a different god behind every bush, one for the hills and another for the valleys, one holding up the sky and yet others shining on them by day in the sun, and by night in the moon and stars. By this worldview, we might imagine in the English translation of Exodus 20:1-3, nothing more than a narcissistic god resenting the attention that other gods get from the people he's done so much to help.

This is not the picture, however, as is made abundantly clear, not only in Genesis 1, but also just a little further on in Deuteronomy 6:4-5, which says, "*Hear, O Israel! The LORD is our God, the LORD is one! "And you shall love the LORD your God with all your heart and with all your soul and with all your might.*"

This brings up an interesting question. What does it mean to love God?

---

[74] Genesis 1; first book, first chapter.

[75] Deuteronomy 30:15.

[76] Proverbs 29:18 Without a prophetic vision the people cast off moral restraint but he who lives by Torah finds (*ESHER*) happiness.

[77] Those capitalized LORD references are the Hebrew word *Yahweh*, meaning Creator.

We might talk about "being in love," which reflects a passionate infatuation causing bouts of euphoria, panic, poor judgment and rash decisions. So… not this.

We might talk about warm affections and feelings of extreme "liking" without romantic attachment. This might be something like what the command commissions, but emotions are fickle things, and Scripture is anything but an advocate of the fickle.

Among people, Christians like to raise the bar and speak of love beyond issues of like and affection. Here, "to love" is to genuinely desire and seek the other's good. If you have children, then you must realize that you can actually find yourself disliking someone a good deal at times and still love them with everything you have. Here we find the Christian adage, "Hate the sin, love the sinner," and Jesus' second greatest commandment *"Love your neighbor as yourself,"*[78] and even a call to "love" strangers.[79] But how would this relate to our love for God? He is both omnipotent (all-powerful) and the source of all Good, so desiring and seeking His ultimate good is kind of silly. There is no lack of goodness or power for having it that leaves space for our wishing goodness upon Him.

There is another meaning, however, in the Hebrew word that stands behind our translation "love." It is the use of the word "love" in covenants. Emotions may come and go, but in ancient covenants between great Lords and lower subjects (Suzerain & Vassal) the subjects were often called upon to love their Suzerain in the practical terms of loyalty and obedience. Not surprising then, if you look up all the places that people are called upon to love the Creator, it almost always speaks of living out His commands, walking in His ways, clinging to Him in perpetual mindfulness of His rightful place in your life. Now it is this that these passages command.

Hebrews 10:31 declares, *"It is a fearful thing to fall into the hands of the living God,"* and just a bit later says, *"our God is a consuming fire."*[80] Those who behold even a portion of His glory fall down before Him,[81] some as if dead,[82] and no man can see "His face" and live.[83] Here, there is real fear, awe, sometimes joy, and not a little reverence. This goes far beyond warm feelings toward total devotion tinged with fear. It is not uncommon for even the faithful to succumb to frustration with God over the tasks He's put before us, the standards He demands we keep, and the mysteries that surround His will and purposes, even if we know He's right. The heart cries out in anguish with several Psalmists, "How long O' Yahweh!"

---

[78] Leviticus 19:18 in the Old Testament.
[79] Deuteronomy 10:19 in the Old Testament.
[80] Hebrews 12:29 in the New Testament.
[81] Abraham in Genesis 17:3, Joshua in Joshua 5:14-15, Ezekiel in Ezekiel 1:28 & 3:23 in the Old testament Matthew, James, and John in Matthew 17:6, and Paul in Acts 9:4 in the New Testament.
[82] Daniel 10:9 in the Old Testament; Revelation 1:9-17 in the New Testament, and several others.
[83] Exodus 33:20 in the Old Testament.

In Exodus 20:1-3 and Deuteronomy 6:4-5, we find the single most basic reality of existence—One God, to Whom we owe everything, Who is to be put first in a world filled with other things that clamor to be first. In addition to calling Deuteronomy 6:4 the greatest of all commandments,[84] Jesus Christ emphasizes the call for priority saying, in Matthew 6:31-33, *"Do not be anxious then, saying, 'What shall we eat?' or 'What shall we drink?' or 'With what shall we clothe ourselves?' For all these things the Gentiles eagerly seek; for your heavenly Father knows that you need all these things. But seek first His kingdom and His righteousness; and all these things shall be added to you."*

When we wake up to the Creator and put Him first in all our doings, the rest of life has a way of working itself out. We can even cry with the tortured saint, Job, "Though He slay me, I will hope in Him."[85]

~Andrew D. Sargent, Ph.D.

---

[84] Matthew 22:36-40 in the New Testament.
[85] Job 13:15 in the Old Testament.

# Reflections & Responses

What does it mean to love?  What misconceptions might we have when we use the word love for many different things and in many other ways?  How does viewing love from the view of an ancient covenant change your thoughts on how we are called to love God and neighbor?

List a few specific changes you think you could make to your daily actions and behaviors to be more in line with these new considerations about the meaning of love as covenant response?

# DAY EIGHTEEN
## Stop Being a Pagan

God gave ten commandments to Abraham's descendants when he created them as the nation of Israel. When followed, these commandments establish a grand vision for God's good life of stability, wisdom, happiness, and wholeness. His first commandment was that they wake up to the One Holy Creator of all and prioritize their lives around Him.

The second command, related to the first, says in Exodus 20:4-5, *"You shall not make for yourself an idol, or any likeness of what is in heaven above or on the earth beneath or in the water under the earth. You shall not worship them or serve them."*

Given the West's love of art, including sculpture, this could seem an alarming command. At this moment, I can see my cast bronze of a bucking bronco who has tossed his rider, a soap stone elephant hollowed out with another inside it. I have a stuffed penguin, a stuffed pig and gorilla, an Army guy, and even a Humanoid asparagus... that veggie has got some tales to tell, I'm sure. All of them are special to me for one reason or another. And this is just my office.

"Those are NOT idols," you say, "We DO NOT worship them," you insist? You are quite correct.

In Israel's experience, however, the lure to idolatry was strong, for all the nations about them were trapped in a pagan worldview. The prophets of Israel had a dickens of a time preventing the Israelites from sliding back into idol worship. The very existence of images was a problem for them... like being a recovering alcoholic who gets a job as a bartender.

But we live in a world where Christianity largely defeated paganism; idol worship is the farthest thing from most people's minds when they see a replica of something, especially when it's crafted in plastics, resins, and stuffed cloth. I don't believe for one second that our art violates this second commandment.

That doesn't mean, however, that we don't violate it in other ways that are more to the point.

It may seem strange to us, but idol worship came with seductive ideas about god, man, and reality, and promised wanton access to sexual delights. In fact, it commanded them. Paganism says you can be "righteous" and still live how you want, because, in paganism, the worshipper served divine powers in ritual in order to get those powers to satisfy the worshipper's own desires. How cool is that?! A god who does what YOU want!!! Sign me up!!!

Just kidding. Don't sign me up... I'll go join the picket line instead.

Here is the rub; idolatry is bigger than worshipping gods through statues. The Word of the Lord in Ezekiel 14:3 describes this phenomenon expertly, saying *"Son of man, these men have set up their idols in their hearts, and have put right before their faces the stumbling block of their iniquity."* The replica is just an object; the idol lives in the pagan heart. Paganism is a worldview, a comprehensive perception of god, man, and reality. The ideas remain, indeed the idols remain, even if the statues change form or have no form.

Paganism, at its heart, uses ritual actions and ritual words to turn the power of a god to fulfill the will of the worshipper. Paganism reduces the idea of god to a function that can be accessed and exploited through man's actions. Christians can even do this by thinking that taking communion, fasting, praying, weeping, or even quoting Scripture at God will get them what they want from God.

When King Saul tries just such a trick with Yahweh (the Creator) in 1 Samuel 15, the Prophet Samuel sets him straight saying in verses 22-23, *"Has the LORD as much delight in burnt offerings and sacrifices as in obeying the voice of the LORD? ...For rebellion is as the sin of divination, And insubordination is as iniquity and idolatry."* In the face of Saul's pagan-minded games, the great Prophet decrees that ritual tricks cannot manipulate the One True God, for He is wholly other than man and invulnerable to human deceit and to their ludicrous attempts at controlling Him.

When Samuel is sent to the boy David's house to anoint King Saul's replacement, he is instantly impressed with David's oldest brother. They didn't even bother bringing David in for the selection. God says to Samuel in 1 Samuel 16:7, *"Do not look at his appearance or at the height of his stature, because I have rejected him; for God sees not as man sees, for man looks at the outward appearance, but the LORD looks at the heart."* 2 Chronicles 16:9 echoes this well, *"...the eyes of the LORD move to and fro throughout the earth that He may strongly support those whose heart is completely His."*

An Idol then, is both more than and less than the carved images against which the verbiage of the 2nd commandment seems rallied. The great preacher A. W. Tozer encapsulated the essence of Idolatry perfectly. I summarize. We are idol worshipers when we look to receive from that which is NOT God, what only God can give. We are idol worshippers when we give to that which is NOT God what only God should receive.

True meaning and purpose are found in God and God's commission in Genesis. Are you, instead, seeking meaning in your race? Your gender? Your career? Your nationality? Are you seeking a satisfaction of soul in sex that can only be found in communion with your Maker? Are you obedient to the cry of substances in defiance of the call of God? Are you willing to cast off God and His commands when they demand that you take a stand against your child? Your spouse? Your family? Your culture?

My bronze bucking bronco is not an idol, but our misaligned commitments just may be. Seek insight from God. He will help you align your soul aright.

~Andrew D. Sargent, Ph.D.

# Reflections & Responses

Consider this particular quote from this chapter in light of your own life:

> The great preacher A. W. Tozer encapsulated the essence of Idolatry
> perfectly. I summarize. We are idol worshipers when we look to
> receive from that which is NOT God, what only God can give. We are
> idol worshippers when we give to that which is NOT God what only
> God should receive.

Examine your life for any area that you are looking to receive what only God
can give. List some potential trouble spots here.

Ask yourself where you might be giving to something/someone what only God deserves. List some areas of potential trouble here.

Idolatry can be sneaky in our hearts, because at our core, we are selfish beings looking for ways to please ourselves. We can look at where we spend our time, treasure, and talents to have a better idea of where our hearts and motivations truly lie. If any of these is out of alignment with God's word, it's time to take a closer look at those things under the microscope of the Bible.

# DAY NINETEEN
## Don't Wear the Name of the Lord in Vain

God founded His good rules for living on ten basic commands. Any people who dedicate themselves to keeping the heart and soul of these commands will find God's good-life... a life of stability, wisdom, happiness, and wholeness... not a perfect life, because people still battle selfishness, and God often transforms us through suffering, but a blessed one.

Now, I say "keeping the heart and soul of these commands" in order to create contrast with the way sinners tend to keep rules... outmaneuvering the intent of rules while giving the vain appearance of being righteous.

Let's consider the third commandment. Exodus 20:7 reads, "*You shall not take the name of the LORD your God in vain, for the LORD will not leave him unpunished who takes His name in vain.*"

When I grew up, kids got their mouths washed out with soap for using vulgar language... even if their parents used it. Believe it or not, however, the worst words on the No No List involved the Father, Son, and Holy Spirit. To take up the name of the Lord as either a swear word, or for no purpose but emotional "filler," was a serious sin.

This included, but was not limited to sound-alikes, like Geeze, GeeWiz, Golly, Golly Gee Wilikers, Gosh, and let's not forget the old standby Gosh Darn it. If we really wanted to outmaneuver the law, we'd shout, "Darn my socks!" What adult could hold us accountable for using darn in its most exacting sense? Did they want to argue with Webster? That certainly didn't work out too well for the Devil![86]

The list got even longer. We had to be careful of terms that referenced God issues like damnation, the cross, and communion wafers... so blasted, bloody, and "Christ on a Cracker" were also out. Don't say these words or allow the spirit that led to them to control your tongue. In fact, I hope you didn't read those aloud... or move your lips when you read silently. I was careful to even type them with my eyes closed so I didn't accidentally think them out loud.

So, as a kid, we felt pretty good about ourselves when we learned to swerve wide of such utterances. We were keeping the third commandment... unlike those loose lipped sows and boars around us. Nothing like a mouth full of Lifebuoy soap to bring on a case of holier-than-thou. Now that lifebuoy is banned in several countries, I'm waiting to get in on the class action lawsuit against the parents of the 70s. Yes, most of us have already inherited everything they had, but it's the principle of the thing.

---

[86] See the story, "The Devil and Daniel Webster," by Stephen Vincent Benét. If you prefer, you can watch the 1936 movie by the same name.

Anyway, getting back to my main point, imagine my dismay when I discovered that there was a lot more to living out the third commandment than avoiding even the appearance of a vain utterance of God's name. There are many circumstances in which we take up the Lord's name in vain without speaking a word.

When I was 18, I was driving my car down Route 495 coming from New Hampshire to my home a little south of Boston. I was doing about 100 mph. Here, "about" means a little over not a little under. I was in a hurry. In my back window, I had a fake vanity plate that had the Christian fish <>< and the letters JESUS. Maybe it was just my own guilty inner voice talking, but I felt like the Lord said sharply, "Slow down! Drive Right! Or take the Jesus plate out of your back window!!!" I am ashamed to say that I immediately pulled over on the highway, removed the Jesus plate, and continued flying south at a little more than a little over 100 mph. Did I mention that I was in a hurry?

We could easily replace this story with those brandishing a "Honk If You Love Jesus" bumper sticker who curse out some blessed driver honking the love of Jesus to them. We could replace it with our bad behavior at work, when everyone knows that we are a believer. Ditto among our neighbors and family.

At 16, I discovered that I could twist my hand inside a soda machine and pop sodas out for free. I didn't think of it as stealing. It was a gift to me for being so cooooool... and a great way to impress my thirsty but poor friends... until my football coach caught me at it that is. He said, "Andrew, what are you doing? Aren't you a Christian? Do Christians steal now?" Suddenly, my explanations of how it wasn't really stealing rang hollow, even in my own ears.

When you read, *"You shall not take the name of the LORD your God in vain,"* Don't just imagine loose lips sinking spiritual ships, hear the words as, "You shall not wear the name of the Lord in such a way that you bring shame on the reputation of the Lord."

Thus, none of us come out of this unscathed. If we truly saw ourselves through God's eyes we'd weep for the unknown ways we shame the name of Jesus by simply "being our bad self" among those who know we are Christians less for our love[87] than for our chitter chatter and Jesus paraphernalia.

Thankfully, in His grace and mercy, God spares us the worst of it, by going gently with us, changing us little by little like a tender father, only giving us a good spanking once in a while when we need it most.

The secret in all this is to respond well to His nudges... His Word... His periodic revelations of us to us... not by taking the Jesus plate out of our rear window, but by leaving it there, slowing down, driving right, and giving a blessing rather than a curse to the guy who drives too slowly in front of us. They are not an obstacle to our purpose, but in Jesus, ARE our purpose.

~Andrew D. Sargent, Ph.D.

---

[87] John 13:35 says, "By this everyone will know that you are my disciples, if you love one another."

# Reflections & Responses

If you have heard the command in Exodus 20:7 in the past. Discuss how this devotion's take on that command differs from how you may have previously read it?

Our new life in Jesus should be reflected in our actions, behaviors, responses and attitudes. Take a moment to reflect on ways that you "wear" the name of Jesus well and list them here.

Are there any areas in your life where if others see you and know you are a Christian might be bringing shame to His name?

# DAY TWENTY
## Sabbath Keeping God's Way

In the Ten Commandments, we find the core of a body of rules for life and society that are God's gift to a floundering race. In them, He reveals the rudiments of the path of life in His world. Today, I want to meditate on the fourth of the great commandments... the keeping of Sabbath.

In Exodus 20:8-11, we read:

> *Remember the Sabbath day, to keep it holy. Six days you shall labor and do all your work, but the seventh day is a Sabbath of the LORD your God; in it you shall not do any work, you or your son or your daughter, your male or your female servant or your cattle or your sojourner who stays with you. For in six days the LORD made the heavens and the earth, the sea and all that is in them, and rested on the seventh day; therefore the LORD blessed the Sabbath day and made it holy.*

There are so many things that deserve attention in these verses, I hardly know where to begin.

The sacred, that which is called upon in terms of "keeping holy" is always a big deal.

It is connected to God's own Sabbath in creation... which is a whole different level of the onion.

Sabbath is about care and concern not just for your own wellbeing, but for the wellbeing of everyone around you, including beasts of burden. It wasn't uncommon to work people to death if you had full power over them, no matter how counterproductive that seems to us.

Also, the giving of the Sabbath to Israel, is made a "covenant sign" for the Moses covenant sworn in Exodus 20-24 and the whole book of Deuteronomy,[88] just as circumcision was the sign of the Abrahamic covenant;[89] covenant signs are always a big deal.

Then we have the issue of what does and doesn't constitute work... a nasty affair in Jesus' day. For instance, "If I find and egg under my chicken at the end of the Sabbath, and I eat that egg, am I participating in the work of the chicken?" And you thought this was going to be just a lot of silly religious talk.

But let's start with the elephant in the room, even if you thought it was just a decorative coat rack. In Scripture, the Sabbath is Friday at sunset to Saturday at sunset. The Jewish people still keep this time slot as their holy Sabbath. In Israel, we watched the sky—three visible stars marked the change.

---

[88] Exodus 31:15-18.
[89] Genesis 17:10-14.

Most Christians, however, revere Sundays midnight to midnight as their "Sabbath day," because Jesus was resurrected on Sunday. Are we Christians being disobedient by doing this? Some groups like the Seventh Day Adventists and Seventh Day Baptists think so. I... reluctantly... think not. My arguments in this regard would prove too much for this devotion, but I'll cut to the heart of it all below.

But first, let's look at the elephant's bigger brother; he's standing in the shadows over there behind the thing you thought was a coatrack. Christians today tend to give very little concern to the issue of work even on their own Sabbath. I had fathered a few children before my own area of the country canceled "the blue laws" and became a 24/7 society. Even before that, however, few concerned themselves with all 39 categories of work disallowed by strict Judaism.[90]

Being gentiles (That's Bible talk for Not-Jewish) we have been called to the New Covenant of Faith in Christ, just as Jewish believers who meet Jesus are, but *without* officially swearing into the Mosiaic covenant.[91] We may grant that Jesus seemed to hate *the way* His fellow Jews kept the Sabbath and the tyrannical expansion of the "letter" of keeping it, with more and more restrictions, niggling over minutia without understanding the heart of keeping it at all. They took that which God gave to them to be a blessing, and turned it into an instrument of oppression.[92] That which God gave to heal, they used to hurt. Jesus was always pushing the envelope on how the religious leaders of His day kept the Sabbath, soooo.... No worries! We were good, right?

But are we? (read that with a really annoying high pitch at the end) I know we're good with ourselves, but doesn't a command of such weight demand some consideration? It's one of the big ten after all. It's saturated in the language of the holy. It connects to our mindfulness of God in creation, and to the call to care for all God's creatures, including those made in His very image. Are we missing out on some blessing that God has for us by being less than attentive to even the idea of a biblical Sabbath?

I think so. I would never want to use some sense of Sabbath LAW to deliver with a curse that which was given to us as a blessing. We live in a 24/7/365 society, for good or ill, and sometimes in order to take care of our own, we have to make hard choices. But imagine taking one day a week to

---

[90] Here is the list: 1. Carrying 2. Burning 3. Extinguishing 4. Finishing 5. Writing 6. Erasing 7. Cooking 8. Washing 9. Sewing 10. Tearing 11. Knotting 12. Untying 13. Shaping 14. Plowing 15. Planting 16. Reaping 17. Harvesting 18. Threshing 19. Winnowing 20. Selecting 21. Sifting 22. Grinding 23. Kneading 24. Combing 25. Spinning 26. Dyeing 27. Chain-stitching 28. Warping 29. Weaving 30. Unraveling 31. Building 32. Demolishing 33. Trapping 34. Shearing 35. Slaughtering 36. Skinning 37. Tanning 38. Smoothing 39. Marking (Orthodox Union, The Melachos Table, https://www.ou.org/holidays/the_thirty_nine_categories_of_Sabbath_work_prohibited_by_law/ (8/15/2023)

[91] Acts 15 tells the tale, as does Colossians 2:1-17.

[92] Mark 2:23-28 and 3:1-6. John 5, 7, and 9.

really rest. Image using that day to focus on family… whether spiritual or physical. Imagine that on that day, you worship, pray, receive instruction from the Scriptures, see your friends, do something to bless others, have people to your home, visit other in theirs… and most importantly, just breathe and think how lucky you are to know the one who made the world, however big of a mess people have made of it. I can't help but think that this just might become the blessing to mind, body, spirit, and community that God meant it to be when he broke into the demanding world of the Ancient Near East with His Sabbath command in the first place.

~Andrew D. Sargent, Ph.D.

# Reflections & Responses

Discuss any previous thoughts you had about the idea of a Sabbath rest?

What are some of your real-world challenges to taking a day of rest?

Discuss any blessings you might anticipate in taking a full day of rest once a week?

If you can't start with a full day, what are some ways you can begin to implement rest into your routine to honor God?

# DAY TWENTY-ONE
## Honoring Those
## Racist, Homophobic, Patriarchal
## People Who Raised You

In the list of rules for society that God gave as a good gift to His confused, rebellious, and self-destructive image bearers, the first to which He attached a promise is *"Honor your father and your mother, that your days may be prolonged in the land which the LORD your God gives you."*[93] Given the nature of these rules, one may ask whether this commandment elicits special blessings from the Creator directly, or merely activates innate blessings woven into His world and your soul.

Answer: "YES!"

If you have any doubts about this "God-obviously-doesn't-know-MY-parents" command, consider how hard tyrants work to break the parent-child bond, seducing children away in a hundred ways to turn them into "useful idiots" who destroy their own families. Even Aristotle noted the pattern. This sits at the soul of our millennia long battle against humanist hopes for Utopia, waged for over a century though the varied seductions of Marxism.[94] The godless exploit every opportunity to turn each generation against previous generations. Doubt me? Just ask your "racist" "homophobic" "transphobic" "patriarchal" parents who don't care enough about the environment and eat meat.

What then is the positive that God lays against so many negatives invented by the subversive to gain power? What is this "honoring" that God thought important enough to include among The Big Ten?

Let's knock out two fictions.

---

[93] Exodus 20:12.

[94] Marxism in all its forms is responsible for all the nonsense happening in our society today. Vulgar Marxism (Socialism, Communism, Class Warfare) based on economics gave way to Critical Marxism which sought to multiply the points of violent resistance for destroying Western Civilization (Feminism, Sexual Revolution, Race Marxism, Socialism) which gave way to Postmodernism which attacked the notion of science, truth, morals, and language as nothing but instruments of power and oppression so as to continue unraveling the West by undermining its ability to speak or exist. This all has now given way to modern Critical Marxism which has multiplied its points of attack even beyond the hopes of early Critical Marxists… (Anti-colonial Marxism, New Waves of Feminism, Environmentalism/climate studies, Gender studies, LGBT+ Agenda, Critical Race Theory, Queer Theory, Fat Studies, Able-ism, Ageism, and the belief that to be part of any demands fighting for them all, and that any combination of them establishes a new category of unquestionable expertise.) No gender, no morals, no limits on declared identities, no cultural norms, no limits on sexual expression, no property, no free markets, and total government to keep enforcing these agendas.

First, Paul quotes our passage and declares in Ephesians 6:1, *"Children, obey your parents because you belong to the Lord, for this is the right thing to do."* This clearly makes obedience an essential part of honoring parents in childhood, but it neither demands obedience from *adult* children nor limits honoring parents to *minor* children. As with civil disobedience, even among children there are times where strict adherence to wicked demands by parents are superseded by commitments to the higher power of Christ.[95] The good news—or bad news if you were hoping to get off the hook on this thing—is that honoring mother and father is bigger than obedience, for adults are called to honor father and mother, and it can be accomplished even in the face of morally necessary resistance.

While so-called *rational people* see family connection as an accident of nature and, thus, nothing to get all worked up about, Christians should see family connection as vital. We should not only believe that God is sovereign (a theological statement acknowledging that God is in complete control), but also that His plan, though often mysterious to us, *"work together for good to them that love God, to them who are the called according to his purpose."*[96] These good purposes are partially represented in the essential command, *"Honor your father and mother."*

Second, Moses survived out of a generation of boys tossed by their parents into the Nile river at Pharaoh's command. He led the mothers and fathers, sisters and brothers of those murdered boys out of Egypt and into the wilderness on their way to the Promised Land. And it was through THIS Moses that God commanded the Children of Abraham to honor their fathers and mothers that their days might be long upon the earth.

Sooooo… what's our excuse for refusing to honor *our* parents?

Some, no doubt, have some horrific stories to tell.

A friend of mine grew up with a single hippie mother who was a practicing witch. She saturated his life in drugs and immorality, and even threw orgies with him in the house, allowing others to abuse him. He found Christ through a church youth ministry and only this kept him sane in the midst of her insanity. When his mother's health began to fail seriously, he wrestled with how he could honor God by honoring his mother without exposing his family to her influence. It grieved him that he did not have the kind of mother that could be a grandmother to his kids. But still, she was his mother, and he wanted to do right by her.

I could tell of another woman whose mother severely abused her and her siblings when they were growing up on a farm. She would beat them 'til their eyes and ears bled. She'd make them kill their pets for displeasing her… and the things she did to those animals if they refused taught them early to put them down mercifully on command. Twice, her father came in from the fields to find that she'd put them all down for naps in their respective bedrooms and set the

---

[95] Mark 3:21, 31-35; Acts 4:1-20, 5:17-29; Daniel 3 & 6.
[96] Romans 8:28.

house on fire. Still, as a Christian, she has labored to make sure that her mother is housed, fed, and cared for.

And what could we say of the dangerous? Sexual predators? Severe addicts? Thieves and liars? All going by the names Mom or Dad? These are hard issues. They need prayerful meditation and wisdom from the Lord. But, somehow, someway, if for nothing other than being the vessels through whom we received life, God has called us to a response of "honor." Thus, we should find gratitude where it can be found rather than drowning our souls in the ugliness and the lack that people without Christ often allow to consume not only their own lives, but the lives of their children as well.

Perhaps some of you are saying, "I've got them beat. Let me tell you about MY parent(s)." To you, I encourage that prayerful mediation. Ponder how you might use the command to honor in order to heal from the tortures your lost parents have laid against you?

Many, however, will feel a touch of shame for the lesser things that they have allowed to crowd out gratitude and to blossom into dishonor. Repent. Restore honor.

I can't tell you what your specific situation may entail, but I can say, that your life will be better if you find a way to honor God by truly honoring what you can honor in your parents.

And if you have good parents, never forget what a blessing they are.

~Andrew D. Sargent, Ph.D.

# Reflections & Responses

Take time today to find a way to take a step to honor your parents. List some things you can do right now to begin living in a more honoring way toward them?

Discuss any serious challenges you face in trying to live out this pattern of honoring relationship with your parents? Is it time to forgive them or heal from them, and let God carry the load you have been carrying concerning them?

If you are in a stage in your life where you parents have already passed, list some ways you can honor them now?

# DAY TWENTY-TWO
## Not Murdering God's Way

In The Ten Commandments, we have the rudiments of a legal code. Torah,[97] however, is much bigger than a legal code. In it, specific commands are woven into the rich context of Israel's covenant living before Holy God. Thus, while a judicial body might hold one accountable to say, Exodus 20:13, "*You shall not murder,*"[98] in terms of whether someone intentionally killed someone or not and for just or unjust cause, their power stops there. Its context in Scripture, however, adds layers. God's desire goes further than whether or not we actually swing the axe. He looks at the heart of the one dreaming about the axe.

A pastor of mine, once asked the room, "What do you think it would take to drive you to murder?" Eager to look both tough and spiritual, people offered up several scenarios, all extreme, in which their Christian heart might be driven to murder. Horrific imaginings indeed. One even pontificated about time travel and meeting up with Hitler as a child.

Me? I said, "Maybe if someone steals my parking spot." It was then that everyone realized that I'd won the game.

Jesus knew that murder doesn't begin with an act of violence; it begins with anger, resentment, envy, jealousy, hurt feelings, consuming greed, frustration, or even contempt for your fellow man. It begins with selfishness run amuck. In Matthew 5:21-22, Jesus says:

> "*You have heard that the ancients were told, 'YOU SHALL NOT COMMIT MURDER' and 'Whoever commits murder shall be liable to the court.' "But I say to you that everyone who is angry with his brother shall be guilty before the court; and whoever shall say to his brother, 'Raca,'[99] shall be guilty before the supreme court; and whoever shall say, 'You fool,' shall be guilty enough to go into the fiery hell.*"

My temper has been a struggle. No bodies in my trunk, but on more than a few occasions there certainly could have been. My heart has touched murder, and even its shadow in my soul has terrified me on a few occasions.

---

[97] First five books of the bible.
[98] The famous reading in the King James Bible renders Exodus 20:13 as "Thou shalt not kill." The Hebrew word used behind "kill," however, does not mean kill; it means murder... the unlawful inexcusable taking of a human life. There are different forms of "killing" that are not only allowed, but demanded in order to maintain Divine Order.
[99] This is an Aramaic term that is a explicative uttered in rage, meaning, "Fool!" or "Worthless Fellow!"

I remember weeping with my mother over a Christmas morning incident in which I smashed a gift I had lovingly and excitedly bought special for my little brother. He hurt me with his contempt for me (a particularly volatile button in my soul) and I lost it. I was upset because I could not undo the damage. But I was more upset, because I knew that I might just as easily have destroyed him for whom I had lovingly and excitedly bought presents.

I've murdered souls without harming a hair. On the last day of elementary school, as my younger brother mounted the bus in joy, he spun to point out a girl in his class whom he'd been ridiculing to me for a while. "That's her! That's her! Doesn't she look ridiculous!" She did. She was one of those unfortunates in looks and mind and social awareness that make "normal people" feel uncomfortable, and make foolish children, who don't know how to deal with such negative emotional responses, torment them. I laughed out loud at the sight of her. Nay, I guffawed. She was mounting the stairs of the bus next to our bus, obviously excited with everyone else that it was the last day of school. She was joyous and sharing a beautiful moment with her classmates, feeling one with the group in a comradery normally denied her. Then she locked eyes with me, pointing, and howling, gleeful scorn etching my entire frame and face. I watched her soul die. I knew in an instant what a horrid thing I'd done, and that I would never be able to undo it. Later, alone, I wept.

Things with my brother got worse after puberty. I was bigger, stronger, faster, better prepared as a fighter, and in a much fouler mood. Again, he incited me to violence. See what I did there? I put part of it on him. From his perspective, he should take part of it onto himself, contemptuously poking a bear, but for my part, I must take it all. I allowed my temper to grow almost beyond my ability to contain it. It was not a blackout rage. I remember it all. I felt murder coursing through my veins; my mind conjured the images of bludgeoning, blood, and death, hands gripping neck, fists cracking bone, rending, tearing, snapping. Thank heaven my older brother and sister were there to protect him. Their very presence gave me strength to restrain my hand. In the full frenzy of my... rage does not capture it... my wrath... no... I know no word in English that satisfies for what I felt... but in the height of it, God broke in and let me see my own murderous heart as He'd done that Christmas... that day on the bus. It broke me. I cried out for divine mercy and more importantly for a divine cleansing... I needed help and begged God for it. He did not disappoint.

It reminded me of part of a poem that goes:

"Once I prayed, I knew not what I said; Show me myself,
oh Lord, alas I did not dread; The hideous sight which now, I
shudder to behold; Because I knew not self-aright; And I was
led in answer to my prayer; As step by step to see my wretched
heart lay bare; Then I prayed: stay, Lord, I cannot bear the

sight; And pityingly His hand was stayed, His hand was stayed."[100]

Many of us have never learned how to properly manage negative emotions and we tend to express this emotional immaturity through anger; many ugly works and words flow out of that anger. This is where murder hides, lurking in wait in our unexamined souls. Bring this to God. Seek self-knowledge from the Holy Spirit. Cry out for divine wisdom from Christ, so that you might develop the character of Jesus.

~Andrew D. Sargent, Ph.D.

---

[100] Helen McDowell, "Once I Prayed." You can read the whole wonderful thing here: https://www.fincher.org/Quotes/Friends.shtml.

# Reflections & Responses

Often the most horrific things start with something that seems benign, or, dare I say, even virtuous. "You do you!" "You do whatever works for you," sounds benign, but when left to ourselves we will find just how selfish and self-centered we really are. Perhaps anger has never been your vice, as it has been for many of us, but jealousy, resentment, and offense can all lead down this same path.

List some areas of your own life that came to mind as you've read and reflected on this devotion. What is He asking you to lay at His feet? What part of your heart needs to bow before him that is currently on the path of murder?

# DAY TWENTY-THREE
## Road Rage, Frustration, & Divine Purpose

Exodus 20:13 gives a simple command with layers of implications in the context of Scripture. *"You shall not murder,"* demands that society punish legally provable murderers with death, and, more deeply yet, that believers pull murder, roots and all, from their souls.

I've been serving the Lord as a full-fledged "I've accepted Jesus into my heart" disciple for 51 years (1972-2023). I was baptized in the Holy Spirit and called into full-time ministry 40 years ago this month (August 1983-August, 2023). I have waged war against my own propensity to "anger" for the whole of it. It has not been a fruitless fight, for I have grown a lot in this area, but neither is it a finished fight.

I call anger, "the monochromatic blaze of multispectral injury." (Because I like big words.) Sometimes what's being injured needs to be injured to provoke personal growth, but anger is still a response to that pain or fear of that pain. That pain may be caused by jealousy (feeling threatened in who you are or what you have), or envy (wanting what someone else has), frustration (the distance between wanting and having), greed (the hunger to have), disappointment (not getting what you want to have), hurt feelings, wounded pride, fear of loss, confusion, guilt… get the idea of multispectral yet?

Women, it is claimed, have more sensitivity to their emotional landscape than men do. I think there is some room for argument there, but they definitely have a great propensity to feeling broadly and complicatedly, and need to examine the deeper reasons for wanting to poison their husband's meatloaf.

Men, however, are often insensible to the subtle details behind their anger; they might not even be able to tell you why they are angry. This lack of introspection may serve them well when defending against invading hoards or combing the country side for tasty critters to feed their families (after their wives have cooked them up in a light garlic butter sauce, naturally), but it is less helpful in coping with the civic duties of not fist fighting with strangers and being attuned the emotional needs of their loved ones.

So here is tip #1: Guys tend to be good at compartmentalizing feelings from tasks, so setting myself the task of understanding my anger when it starts to rise or when its abatement delays gives me something intentional to do. For Example: "My feelings are hurt because I want this person to love me with all their heart, but they seem to be showing contempt for me." This puts the whole matter in another perspective. "Dearest One, I love you with the red hot passion of a thousand suns, but when you did this, it hurt me, because I felt unloved." This does far more good than my more Neanderthal reactions. You can fill in all the blanks for your own situation.

Several years back, my window for seeing a particular film was short. My third child, my sweet Tigger of a girl, asked if I could pick up her friend and take them both to her house near the theater. Her friend delayed and delayed and delayed. I found my temper rising. I didn't want to miss my movie. I was curt with them both. When we hit traffic, my anxiety started to rise exponentially. I began to bicker at these kids for their inconsiderate treatment of my time. And just when I was really ready to let 'em have it… I saw myself. I call it "God turning a mirror on me." Was a stupid movie really worth all this anger, all this turmoil? I apologized to them and explained my frustration. I took them out for ice cream before dropping them off and heading home smiles all around.

Tip #2: When you feel yourself getting worked up. Stop and ask yourself, "Is this issue, really so important that it is worth the emotional trauma that my anger is causing?" "Can my anger fix this?" 999 times out of 1000, the answer should be NO! Ah! But stopping. There's the rub. Ask God for help.

Everything between point A and point B feels to me like a waste of time.

Tip #3: In terms of driving, pursuing personal development through books or courses on tape (Tape? How old am I?) has helped with time frustrations on the road. Delays are often nothing more to me now than a few more chapters or another lecture.

Still, people who get in my way when I am pursuing point B, can easily become an object for my anger, even if only internally. Why won't they just get out of my way! Why can't they just do their JOB!!!

Tip #4: I've developed the habit of telling myself, "People are NOT an obstacle to my purpose. In Christ, they ARE my purpose." It is surprisingly shaming and immensely helpful.

On to road rage. I am forgiving of unintentional flubs. I am annoyed by slowness. I am provoked by stupidity. Drivers who show disdain for the impact that their driving has on others, however, really burn my bonnet. I become overwhelmed with such righteous indignation (not necessarily shared by the Lord, Himself, mind you) that I know that I must punish them. My older brother helped me out here.

Tip #5: From my brother, Greg: "When someone does something that really gets me angry on the road. I ask myself to recall a time where I, for one reason or another, did something just as stupid to someone else." This is better than waving at other drivers with fewer fingers than a good Christian should, and it cools the spirit with a form of self-compassion extended to someone else.

There are times to be righteously angry. Our own anger seldom earns that label. Whatever your poison when it comes to wrath, it is important to address it in the Lord, for He has called His children to be instruments of His love in the world.

~Andrew D. Sargent, Ph.D.

# Reflections & Responses

When dealing with the beast of anger, one additional tip that can be helpful is when you feel the internal temperature rising, step away and pray God's word. Find a Scripture is particularly helpful to you given your temperament and post it everywhere as a reminder to keep your cool. When you seek God in your time of anger, He will meet you; and each time He meets you, and you allow Him, He will change you to be a little more like Him. Some helpful scriptures to keep handy are Psalm 141:3; Psalm 37:8; Ecclesiastes 7:9; James 1:19-20, and many more. When you have time look each one up and respond here with thoughts and questions.

# DAY TWENTY-FOUR
## What's Sex Got to Do with It?

The seventh of the Big Ten commandments, given by our loving Creator to bless us with a special revelation of the path of life that He wove into the fabric of His good world, is a blessed torment. It strikes at the heart of being creatures who by divine design were made for sex and reproduction. God's first words over man in Genesis 1:28 were a blessing, saying, "Be fruitful and multiply and fill the earth." Then, in Exodus 20:14, He goes and complicates everything by commanding, "You shall not commit adultery."

Just kidding... God complicated it right off the bat by the very nature of the creation of male Adam and female Eve as the start of the human family. [101] In Moses' divine commentary on Adam's glorious Ode to Woman, [102] we read, "Therefore a man shall leave his father and his mother and hold fast to his wife, and shall become one flesh." [103] Jesus tacks on, "So they are no longer two but one flesh. What therefore God has joined together, let not man separate." [104]

The pattern of creation itself is instructive. God made Adam and Eve, not Adam and Steve, or mankind wouldn't have gone very far. Further yet, God made Adam and Eve, not Adam and Eve and Indira and Yolanda and Miriam and Sofia. God intends that our sexuality be funneled into the creation of a family through the preservation of marriage—husband and wife in a lifelong, exclusive, one-flesh union. [105]

The problem is that chastity, monogamy, and sexual fidelity are difficult. Just as we need to eat, but must eat the right things in the right portions lest we suffer physical harm, our sexuality must be properly channeled lest we become soul sick. Sex is a drive not a need, but it is a powerful drive... easily perverted by selfishness.

I (Andrew) once had a sky-diving friend who described his exploits as "better than sex." I just figured he wasn't doing it right. I've never jumped out of a plane, but I cannot imagine a greater exhilaration than sex. It is glorious fire in our bones, celestial electricity in our veins. Our bodies pine for sex. Thus, those who have lived in sexual wantonness can scarce imagine that

---

[101] Genesis 2.

[102] Genesis 2:23: Then the man said, "This at last is bone of my bones and flesh of my flesh; she shall be called Woman, because she was taken out of Man." The Hebrew manifests great excitement on the part of Adam when first he meets his counterpart. Her eyes are fewer, but much nicer than the spiders.

[103] Genesis 2:24.

[104] Matthew 19:6.

[105] There is a discussion to be had about God's tolerance for certain forms of polygamy during the Old Testament era, but it was never God's design for man. It was a gracious concession for protecting and sustaining vulnerable women in a sin ravaged world.

sexual restraint is either good or possible. Wanting and not having is a suffering that those unaccustomed to such discipline cannot imagine enduring.

I (Amy) have had many conversations with women who say something akin to, "Yeah, sex is great, but..." or "Sex is great when..." For women sex is great when intimacy is deep. Sex is great but what we really crave is emotional connection. For women sex is a pleasurable piece of a big picture—Making love to her man in their shared "house of dreams," safe, secure, valued. Many woman with emotional damage think that giving themselves over to the erotic desires of various men, imitating the wantonness of the men she's had the unfortunate cause to meet, proves her desirability... that it will bring her the intimate connection that her broken soul craves.

I (Andrew) encouraged pre-marital chastity to my high school mates and lived it... though I had to white-knuckle it on more than a few occasions. I still remember one conversation with a friend, who had yet to "bag a girl," but plotted little else. He referenced my "hang-ups" about sex with sneering tones... my "inhibitions." I told him that morals were not "hang-ups" or "inhibitions" that needed curing with wanton exploration, which actually damages our capacity for lifelong intimate union. Sex is a beautiful God-given drive that flourishes in the right context and rends lives and souls in the wrong context. The very spirit of "bagging a girl" was, I said, disgusting and sad, devoid of soul, and a hopeless path for finding true love. [106] Back then, even my non-Christian friends hoped for a lifelong union with "The One." Unfortunately, they thought they should use a host of 'not-the-one's for their own self-gratification while they looked for the one.

As with almost every other area of life, however, self-control over one's sexual urges is freedom not slavery. It is freedom from being driven about by lust... freedom from hurting, betraying, and neglecting those you love in order to sate your own passions. It is freedom to build something beautiful with a lifelong partner, that blesses those connected to it for generations, be they their children, their children's children, their children's children's children, or the many witnesses to God's plan for man being exemplified in that hard-won union. You are never free until you are free from having to please yourself at other people's expense.

This plan for a couple to become a family, and their family to become families, becoming yet more families is not just difficult in terms of self-control, but it is hard in terms of joining male with female. When I was young, puzzling over the "battle of the sexes," and the struggle for not just a one-flesh union, but the one-soul union that it points toward, I often imagined... respectfully, of course... that this hope was a cosmic joke by God on man. The great spookster Stephen King has noted, "For men, I think, love is a thing formed of equal parts lust and astonishment. The astonishment part women understand. The lust part they only think they understand." Indeed, one social

---

[106] For the record let it be known that I did NOT in fact say, "To Blathe!" Furthermore, no MLT ever competed successfully with true love.

theorist has posited that if women thought about sex the way men tend to think about sex, the world would blow up and that if men thought about sex the way women tend to think about sex the world would shrivel up.

In truth, all the differences between men and women prove a source of great conflict, but God has arranged His world so that the seemingly impossible lifelong, exclusive union of male and female demands that each rise above themselves to meet and love the other on the other's terms. The very act is transformative, giving life not just to children, which almost any heterosexual union can do, but to happy families and societies.

In this present age, it seems more than likely that you, Dear Reader, have failed to live up to God's divine order through pre-marital chastity and/or marital fidelity. There is nothing that can be done about the past save repenting of its mistakes, learning its lessons, and setting the will that from this point forward, with God's grace, things will be different.

Pray therefore, "Lord, help me find your blessed path for my sexuality, so that I, enduring the pain of moral restraint, might experience the joy that You have for me. May I be a positive example for others of the freedom and happiness that can be found in Jesus Christ."

~Andrew D. Sargent, Ph.D.
& Amy S. Kinder, M.A.

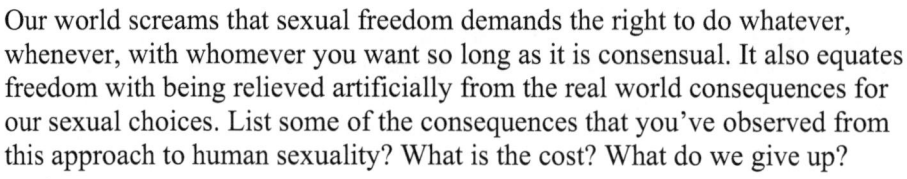

# Reflections & Responses

Our world screams that sexual freedom demands the right to do whatever, whenever, with whomever you want so long as it is consensual. It also equates freedom with being relieved artificially from the real world consequences for our sexual choices. List some of the consequences that you've observed from this approach to human sexuality? What is the cost? What do we give up?

Discuss any benefits you imagine one might enjoy when living out God's design for sex?

# DAY TWENTY-FIVE
## Thou Shalt NOT &
## The Christian Celebration of God's Gift of Sexuality

The 7th commandment says, in Exodus 20:14, "You shall not commit adultery." It, like "You shall not murder," is a spike in a metaphorical wall upon which you can legitimately hang many associated ideas. Not only are overt, legally-punishable sins like murder and adultery the product of internal, legally-unpunishable sins like hate, greed, envy and lust, but they also speak to sins like assault and vandalism, fornication, immodesty, and exhibitionism.

There are two seemingly opposite sinful reactions to divine law. I shall call them "Conniving Legal-loophole Seeker" and the "Unthinking Legal-barrier Maker." The rebellious always seek to rationalize around a command. The other exchanges obliterating rule adherence for wise faithfulness.

One night in Youth Group when I was in High School, we asked our youth leader, Randy, (A hilariously ironic name for the occasion), how much we could do with our girlfriends and boyfriends physically without it counting as sin. He said, "I think, in asking the question, you've already crossed that line. A heart that wants to get as close to sin as it can without being technically guilty of sin, or, perhaps, just escaping the accusation of sin, is wholly unpleasing to the Lord. And that IS sin." We knew he was right, but it frustrated us. We wanted. We wanted badly, and a legitimate slaking of that thirst in marriage was still years away. We were being Conniving Legal-loophole Seekers.

When I was a kid my father put some thick cardboard barrels in our basement with labels on them suggesting that the contents were acidic and could give you a chemical burn. My father, probably trying to be funny, or just tricking us into leaving his project alone, told us not to touch the barrels or the barrels themselves would hurt us. He showed us the scary pictures slapped on the side. My siblings were careful to avoid them. I wouldn't even go in the basement lest I accidentally brush against them and melt my hand like that poor guy on the label. I was being an Unthinking Legal-barrier Maker.

When Conniving Legal-loophole Seekers read, "You shall not commit adultery," their minds go to work preserving as much wiggle room for scratching their sexual pre-marital or extra-marital itches without guilt or shame. We have "progressive" "Christians" who say things like, "this command doesn't say anything about sex before marriage, just adultery." Then they throw in their public support for fornication, living together before marriage, and easy divorce. This is, of course, a shallow reading of the ten commandments in the context of the Torah[107] or Tanakh[108] or Bible, but they

---

[107] The first five books of Moses.
[108] Torah, Prophets, and Writings… i.e. What we call the Old Testament.

find room to skirt the issues whenever Scripture impinges on their passions. "Jesus is about love and mercy not law and judgment! God understands our needs and weakness after all." Some even seek to carve out divine blessing on homosexual sex from Scripture. They believe that the path of life is found within and they don't need some dusty old book telling them how to find it outside themselves through oppressive rules.

When Unthinking Legal-barrier Makers read "You shall not commit adultery," they decide that sex itself must be tainted. Human wanting is to them a spiritual disease that needs to be cut off at the ankles. Taking pleasure in the beauty of the most beautiful of God's creation—women—must be shamed and decried, as should seeking to be as pretty as possible. Arousal in and of itself is dirty, sometimes even in marriage if the desire is strong enough. It was not uncommon in some places back in the day to hear it said of Adam's and Eve's fall into sin, "The problem wasn't the apple in the tree it was the pair in the bush." As with all issues, these folks struggle with tensions and have no skill with wisdom. Everything for them must be a toggle switch of right (click) or wrong (click) and seeking context and paths of spiritual wellness in the complex daily affairs of being human is just too difficult. It's so much easier to just condemn the whole thing and have done with it.

I attended a men's conference at 16. It was on sexual purity. When we broke up into discussion and prayer groups, one of the men in my group asked for prayer that God would take away his desire for his wife. He was plagued with wanting her and knew he just couldn't become the man God wanted him to be so long as sexual passions coursed through him. If my face displayed my mind then these men saw a twisted visage of open-mouthed, wide-eyed wonder at profound idiocy. Even at that age, I wanted to slap the guy upside the head, screaming, "Sex is a good gift from a loving creator to His beloved creatures!!! You are SUPPOSED TO BE PASSIONATE for your wife!!!"

Sex is a good gift from a loving creator!!! The wise know this and seek paths of blessing in it. He also knows, however, that anything as powerful as the sex drive can be twisted in the hands of corrupt hearts. Human selfishness, if it is gifted at anything, shows a particular talent for debasing the beautiful things of God and taking that which was meant as a mechanism for abundant life and turning it into an instrument of oppression, ruin, and death.

God designed us as biological creatures with strong sex drives and made sex one of the most pleasurable experiences one can have in life. There is blessing in it, and we must not scorn His properly-used gift with shame. But according to His plan, our sexuality leads to spreading human thriving only in the context of exclusive lifelong unions of man and wife. Let us strive for God's best by both accepting the blessing and preserving it from perversion.

~Andrew D. Sargent, Ph.D.

# Reflections & Responses

Considering God's design for sex, how do you need to change the way you think about and pursue sexual satisfaction or desire for intimacy?

Singles: All of your sexual behaviors (in thought and action) impact the kind of spouse you are able to become. What steps can you take going forward to secure a God-centered, exclusive, life-long, one-flesh soul-intimate union?

Paul says in Ephesians 5:20-33 …giving thanks always and for everything to God the Father in the name of our Lord Jesus Christ, submitting to one another out of reverence for Christ. Wives, submit to your own husbands, as to the Lord. For the husband is the head of the wife even as Christ is the head of the church, his body, and is himself its Savior. Now as the church submits to Christ, so also wives should submit in everything to their husbands. Husbands, love your wives, as Christ loved the church and gave himself up for her… In the same way husbands should love their wives as their own bodies. He who loves his wife loves himself. For no one ever hated his own flesh, but nourishes and cherishes it… "Therefore a man shall leave his father and mother and hold fast to his wife, and the two shall become one flesh." …let each one of you love his wife as himself, and let the wife see that she respects her husband.

Husbands: (Wives, pay attention to your own question.) Are you loving your wife the way that Christ loves the church? (Ephesians 5:25) Are you laying dow your life for her? What does that look like in your sexual life with your wife? How are you meeting your wife's needs on her terms?

Husbands: Ask your wife how you can better meet her needs. Write her response here:

Wives: (Husbands, pay attention to your own question.) This is a touchy subject for "today's woman," but are you submitting to and respecting your husband as the Scripture instructs? Are you meeting your huband's needs on his terms?

Ask your husband how you can better meet his needs.  Write his response here:

How does following God's precepts for loving our spouse enrich our sex lives?

# DAY TWENTY-SIX
## Let Him Who Steals, Steal No Longer

We are eight commandments into the Big Ten. These God gave for the creation of a stable and blessed society. Exodus 20:15, says simply, *"You shall not steal."* Amazingly enough, however, many worldview assumptions exist inside those four words.

In the book, *The Kite Runner*, Baba, the narrator's father, delivers an insightful speech on theft:

> "...there is only one sin, only one. And that is theft. Every other sin is a variation of theft. ...when you kill a man you steal a life. You steal a wife's right to a husband, rob his children of a father. When you tell a lie, you steal someone's right to the truth. When you cheat, you steal the right to fairness."[109]

In this vein, *"You shall not steal"* is a command to give others their due, whether it regards their person or property, rights as a human being, or simply the civic privileges owed to citizens in good standing.

To fully unpack this idea, we need some sense of what a right is and what one has a right to. Denouncing "Stealing X's right to Y" demands that we understand the basis of rights. Who gave them? Who is to judge their violation? What should those judgments entail? Scripture details all these things.

Westerners tend to run around yelling, "I have rights!" "I have a right to this!" "I have a right to that!" They are quick to insist that some opinion, or word, or action by others, some failing of circumstances, or even the necessity to work for what they want, has robbed them of some "right." Let me just say, "Whoa! Bessy." "Hold the phone on that!" "Not so fast, Jeeves!"

People can claim rights all day long, like my kids used to do, but in the real world yelling "Dibs!" or "Shotgun," doesn't secure rights, and being first to touch your nose doesn't excuse you from honoring them. Rights have to be bound in something real... because the "right" of one person is a divine or legal obligation on another.

Natural rights, for instance, come from God and are rooted in the basic responsibilities that one image bearer of God has toward another image bearer of God *because* he or she IS an image bearer of God. These are "negative rights"... rights for a person and his or her property to be left unmolested, undamaged, alive and free. The only way that one forfeits such rights is by violating someone else's and falling afoul of divinely mandated government, which according to the Apostle Paul "...*does not bear the sword for nothing.*

---

[109] Khaled Hosseini, *The Kite Runner*, (London: Bloomsbury, 2003), pg. 17-18.

*For he is the servant of God, an avenger who carries out God's wrath on the wrongdoer.*"[110]

To lay claim, therefore, to "goods and service rights," for instance—free food, medical care, housing, clothes, etc—demands that someone else be robbed of "natural rights" by being forced to pay for, or otherwise provide, those goods and services.[111]

Living in society may require that some of our freedoms are willingly curtailed in order to reap the rewards of being in a society, (like taxes to pay for public administration, military defense, criminal justice systems, public services open to all citizens in good standing) but neither government agent nor neighbor nor foreign invader has the right to strip away these rights without divine justification through the rule of just law, even if they have the power to do so. Anything less and anything more is theft.

I may claim that I have not stolen anything in my adult life.[112] I am not a thief and, apart from a couple of incidents in my youth before the age of 17, I am innocent of the dark charge. This, however, is a shallow boast when the full nature of theft reveals itself to me in the mirror of Scripture… indeed, when it reveals itself *in* me as I am reflected ill against that perfect measure.

All of the Big Ten commandments are encompassed in "*You shall not steal.*"

If there is One Holy Creator of all, then everything belongs to Him and to deny that claim is theft. Idolatry is giving to that which is not God what only God has a right to receive—Theft! To take up God's name in doings that discredit His reputation among men is to rob God of the glory due His name—Theft!

Have we stolen honor from parents and robbed society by our poor example for others who catch our rebellion like a virus and go on to do yet more harm?[113]

Both fornication (sex before marriage) and adultery (sex that breaks the one flesh union of marriage) steal away a spouses right to true fidelity and robs society of the stability obtained through faithful unions.

To lie in court is to steal away justice, property, and, perhaps the freedom or even the life of the accused. To lie in order to set a guilty man free steals the right of society to protect itself from that person's injustice. To lie generally about others steals truth, mars reputations, and breaks relationships.

One can steal peace, joy, trust, and confidence through the sowing of fear and threat, and through acts of physical and emotional violence. Envy and jealousy, lust and pride, sloth, wrath, and greed when put to work have ruined

---

[110] Romans 13:4.

[111] Charity is another beast altogether. In charity, one willingly and happily gives up that which is his right, to bless another. This is a great principle for a covenant heart, but its soul dies beneath the law-maker's gavel.

[112] I have told the tale of my Orange Soda exploits previously, and will tell of my battle with covetousness further on.

[113] Exodus 21:15, 17; Deuteronomy 21:18-21; See also Proverbs 20:20.

lives, tanked careers, fostered instability, eroded meaning and purpose, and severed sacred bonds—Theft!

The Apostle Paul gives some practical commands regarding thieves in Ephesians 4:28, saying *"Let him that stole steal no more: but rather let him labor, doing honest work with his own hands, so that he may have something to give to anyone in need."* We have stolen many things in life that we can neither return nor restore, but Paul calls for a flip in orientation from being a taker to being a giver, from being sloppy and indolent to being industrious and attentive.

In Jesus Christ, there is mercy where there is confession and repentance. But it all begins with seeing one's self in the mirror of God's word. *"You shall not steal!"*

~Andrew D. Sargent, Ph.D.

# Reflections & Responses

As you reflect on the devotions expansive ways of thinking about stealing, list some ways that the commandment "Thou shall not steal" rings differently for you?

List the things that you have stolen in your life, and be sure to include things that you are currently stealing?

Take time to pray and confess these things today. Respond to Paul's call to turn from being a taker to being a giver in the area you have confessed to the Lord today.

# DAY TWENTY-SEVEN
## Possession, Charity, & The Christian Spirit

We've been exploring the Ten Commandments and, by now, I'm hoping you've seen a distinct pattern in our meditations on them. We've articulated the value of these commandments as agents of legal structure in a blessed society AND explored them as agents of instruction for the covenant heart of the worshipper.[114] Both roles are important.

Even taken at their most exacting literalism, the Ten Commandments prove essential for a stable society. Imagine living in a world where people took one day a week to both rest and give rest to others... where they honored their parents, never murdered, or stole, or defiled their marriages. Imagine a world where everyone could be wholly trusted in legal disputes. This would be like heaven on earth. Of course it is an impossible world if people don't have a moral foundation for such behaviors... like a commitment to the One Holy Creator of all who laid down such rules, lived with an awareness of how their every action reflected poorly or well on His name, and having a decided aversion to pagan and godless thinking.

Then imagine how such things, if kept as a code for society, would bleed into social expectations. Not murdering becomes an anchor for learning to love one's neighbor and for properly handling anger, envy, or resentment when they arise and not merely when they look to boil over into violence, theft, or vandalism. Denouncing adultery becomes an anchor for general sexual restraint and the common recognition that each is born to be the spouse of another from the start... so that pre-marital chastity is honored as the foundation of marital fidelity that it is. Honesty in court becomes an anchor for truthfulness in all of one's dealings.

Anything that speaks to the governance of society becomes political, because politics are the ideas involved in establishing and administering the policies of community. Saying that men are happiest when they are as free as possible within the confines of a safe and prosperous community is a political statement. When the Ten Commandments declare *"You shall not steal,"* in Exodus 20:15 that too is a political statement.

Like the other commands, *"You shall not steal,"* as we've previously noted, becomes an anchor for the covenant heart of the worshipper to give every soul their due as befits image bearers of the One Holy Creator. But it goes further yet. The very idea of stealing rests on a political foundation of

---

[114] "The covenant heart of the worshipper" is the heart of the individual that recognizes that he or she is bound in covenant to the Lord, to obey His commands, imitate His character, help fulfill His mission, and allow His Holy Spirit to transform him or her into the likeness of Jesus Christ.

property rights; it's in the definition of "steal." Just as the creation is the possession of the Creator, so the produce of an image bearer is his or hers.

When you mention property rights today, many scoff, "Yeah, rich people are always worried about property rights!" But the right to own and for what one owns to be left unmolested by others is actually the hope of the poor. It is the great incentive to labor. You work; you earn; you control what you earn and you control what you buy with what you earn. It is also the soul-discipline of the poor, driving them to honest labor and not to seek easy attainment, calling them to emulate and not envy.

Even in the New Testament, we find Jesus addressing divine grace and mercy through the parabolic vineyard owner, *"Friend, I am doing you no wrong. Did you not agree with me for a denarius? Take what belongs to you and go. I choose to give to this last worker as I give to you. Am I not allowed to do what I choose with what belongs to me? Or do you begrudge my generosity?"*[115] These are powerful ownership statements for both the vineyard owner's claims of rights of possession and his declaration of what is owed and, thus, owned by the workers who made a verbal contract for labor with him.

Even in the very context of a community that has shocked everyone by willingly giving what is theirs freely available to help the needy among them, Peter says, *"Ananias, why has Satan filled your heart to lie to the Holy Spirit and to keep back for yourself part of the proceeds of the land? While it remained unsold, did it not remain your own? And after it was sold, was it not at your disposal? Why is it that you have contrived this deed in your heart? You have not lied to man but to God."*[116] This man and his wife are cursed because they boasted of giving it all when they had, in point of fact, kept some back, NOT *because* they held some back. The need was great. The social pressure for generosity great. But Peter defends property rights to the bitter end.

Ready for this to get tricky? As a political statement, *"You shall not steal,"* is a vital foundation stone for a free and prosperous society. As an anchor for the covenant heart it demands that the worshipper give others their due and curb their own actions to respect the divinely set boundaries of others.

But it goes further yet, for our ownership of that which we have produced or earned is an iron spike driven into a wall that is wholly owned by God Himself. We are, therefore, stewards of what we have produced or earned in His world. In this position, as stewards, we are called to reflect the character of God in how He deals with what He ultimately owns.

It is in this context that He calls upon His covenant children to defend property rights as a necessary foundation for community, to give every soul their due, and to personally, with a free will and total stewardship control, share His generous heart. Go forth, therefore, and do all three.

~Andrew D. Sargent, Ph.D.

---

[115] Matthew 20:13-15.
[116] Acts 5:3-4.

# Reflections & Responses

This chapter focuses on layers and tensions. List some ways so far that seeing the Ten Commandments as law AND principles for the covenant heart have challenged the way you think of your own life in community.

We might not be able to change the whole world, but often we can change "our world" by changing ourselves. List some ways you imagine your own life would change if you implemented these Ten Commandments in your own life?

How does the tension between property rights and stewardship challenge your mindset in dealing with all that you have, with all that others have, and your responsibility for both self-limiting to respect other's rights and wisely "open-handed" and merciful like God is?

# DAY TWENTY-EIGHT
## Live Not By Lies… or Malicious "Truth"

God has given humanity ten social anchors for sustaining prosperous and free societies. We call these the Ten Commandments. As anchors they are more than just enforceable laws for society, they are principles of existence tethered to laws for society, which should shape our every interaction. In Exodus 20:16, we find the ninth. It says, *"You shall not bear false witness against your neighbor."*

Now, the word "witness" seems to concern court situations. "Witness" seems to carry the weight of texts like Deuteronomy 19:15, *"A single witness shall not suffice against a person for any crime or for any wrong in connection with any offense that he has committed. Only on the evidence of two witnesses or of three witnesses shall a charge be established."* So, the ninth commandment, at its most basic, speaks to the necessity for a trustworthy legal system in which testimony in any case can rightly be used to establish justice, acquitting the innocent and punishing the guilty.

In its larger context, however, it preaches honesty to the covenant heart of the worshipper.[117]

A "hermeneutic" is the body of rules and attitudes used to interpret anything as you engage it. In terms of shared social values, we may speak of a "hermeneutic of love" vs. a "hermeneutic of violence" forming the foundation of a culture.

A "hermeneutic of love" is built on a fundamental engagement of others through trust until given a reason not to trust. We engage others to understand them, to learn from them, to connect with them, to find mutual benefit in each other. People are regarded as essentially truthful and well-meaning unless proving otherwise. Believe it or not, this describes most of Western Civilization, built as it is on a biblical worldview, where honesty is a core value. Individuals may defy this, but the whole of society has tended toward it. We are shocked and disgusted by encounters with the disingenuous.

In a hermeneutic of violence, others, particularly strangers, are approached with skepticism first and must give clear reason to be trusted. People are assumed to be plotting and dishonest, seeking an advantage and saying whatever they need to say to get the upper hand. They engage others not to understand them or to connect with them, or to learn from them, and definitely not to find mutual benefit. Rather, we seek in every encounter to out argue them or outmaneuver them, to best them, to gain at their loss. This describes most of

---

[117] "The covenant heart of the worshipper" is the heart of the individual that recognizes that he or she is bound in covenant to the Lord, to obey His commands, imitate His character, help fulfill His mission, and allow His Holy Spirit to transform him or her into the likeness of Jesus Christ.

the world outside of Western Civilization built as it is on ages old paganism of one form or another. It is also the future of our nation, if we allow our Judeo-Christian roots to continue to erode before the hermeneutic of violence employed by social/critical Marxism... i.e. Critical theory.

In a society characterized by honesty in its dealings, a hermeneutic of love is a great advantage, speeding up processes, and allowing a free flow of cooperation in achieving mutually beneficial ends. Yes, criminals will find many easy marks in such a place,[118] so, even there, the wise remember, "In God we trust, all others we verify."

In a society characterized by dishonesty, a hermeneutic of love faces many challenges. The best we can do is to be wholly honest ourselves and ever wary of the fact that others are not. When enough people embrace the joys of honesty, however, cultures and the masses in them begin to change.

Scripture, anchored in commands like, "*You shall not bear false witness against your neighbor*," strives to create societies in which we love our neighbors like ourselves, seek mutual benefit, or even favor the benefit of the other in charity. A place where we speak truth to them and about them, hoping for harmony in community and honesty in all our dealings.

Is there, however, such a thing as being TOO honest? Yes… and No.

My wife, Melodie, spent her 16th summer in Haiti digging rubble to supply stones for a new church edifice there. One of the members of her team went around all summer telling each person the most ruthless and unkind "truths" that he could come up with about them, whether it was how unflattering an outfit looked, how fat or skinny he thought you were, or even how dumb or ugly or boring one struck him. In each instance of wounded pride, hurt feelings, or raging disgust, he would put his palms in the air like an innocent and declare, "I'm just being honest. God wants us to be honest."

In 2002, a visitor to my church walked up to me while I was chatting with some of the elders and deacons and handed me a note. He asked me to hand it to one of the men standing beside me, but not to read it. He stood waiting. To his annoyance, I opened it without passing it on and read, "You are a fat slob and an embarrassment to the name of Christ." I turned to him angrily and said, "What is wrong with you?" He said, "As believers we must speak truth."

Hmmmm… is gossip and the delivery of unsought malicious opinion truth telling??? I think not.

And what are we to do if "Neo-Nazi's" come to our door and demand to know where we are hiding the people they want to murder? Should we spill the beans and pride ourselves on our honesty?

What are we to do when our wives ask us if that dress makes them look fat… and it does?

These, and many things like them, are matters to work out through a wrestling match between our conflicting, but noble, social goals, consciences,

---

[118] Isaiah 26:10 says, "*If favor is shown to the wicked, he does not learn righteousness; in the land of uprightness he deals corruptly and does not see the majesty of the LORD.*"

and Scripture. Even so, it is Gods design in commands like, "*You shall not bear false witness against your neighbor,*" to build an honest society where truth reigns lovingly to establish and maintain sincere bonds of community.

Let us pray, "Lord, teach me to live honestly in all my dealings, and give me the wisdom to do so in a way that both pleases you, and builds up a community of neighborly love."

~Andrew D. Sargent, Ph.D.

# Reflections & Responses

List some ways that your society would change if its people were to follow a hermeneutic of love and justify it?

List some ways that your society would change is its people were to adopt a hermeneutic of violence?

Discuss a few sticky situations that you've encountered where commitments to being honest and truly loving have seemed in tension. How did you handle them? If there are ways that this devotion has challenged your past handling of them, make note of them.

# DAY TWENTY-NINE
## The Day I Beat Kleptomania & Became an Honest Man

The last of the great commandments given by God to Israel at Mount Sinai in order that they might reap the benefits of a blessable and blessed society cuts below the surface of the previous four commandments in a powerful way. It strikes at the underground spring from which many sinful acts are fed. Exodus 20:17 says, *"You shall not covet your neighbor's house; you shall not covet your neighbor's wife, or his male servant, or his female servant, or his ox, or his donkey, or anything that is your neighbor's."* Where Exodus 20:13-16 forbids murder, adultery, theft, and deceit,[119] Exodus 20:17 says, "And don't even think about them either!" "kill the root."

I was four when I defeated the temptation to steal. This doesn't mean that I never stole anything again, twice more in my life before the age of 17, I would have to reconsider my definitions of "theft" and repent, but on that day, I killed something hideous in my soul and, thus far, it has stayed dead.

My mother had brought me and my three siblings to a stranger's house, and we spent the day on their front porch digging through their kids' toy box and playing. I took a fancy to this little rubber guy on a matchbox motorcycle. I wasn't interested in the bike, just the guy. I liked the colors, the way it felt and flexed, his helmet and uniform. I wanted it... badly.

When you want something badly that isn't yours and that craving becomes all-consuming, and your emotions wage war against your conscience with excuse after excuse for why its only right for you to take it, to do it... it is almost NEVER the right thing to do. Nay, let me bold. A nagging desire at war with conscience is NEVER the right thing to do. It may be your desires or your conscience that needs addressing, but it is never right to side with passion over conscience.

I am uncertain how long we actually played on that porch... it seemed an age to me... perhaps it felt longer because of my own internal struggle... but I do know that I spent that time putting the little guy in my pocket, taking it out to gaze upon it, tossing it back into the toy box, digging it out again to gaze upon it again before putting it back into my pocket... over and over and over again.

I knew it was wrong to take it. I don't know how I knew it was wrong. I can't recall ever getting a specific lesson on theft, though I must have slept through a few different sermons on the matter in Church... maybe there were lessons in Sunday School, though I don't remember any. Still, somehow, I knew that it wasn't mine, that it belonged to another, that it would be a

---

[119] We've already discussed how deep and wide these commands are by way of the cultivation of a covenant heart for the Creator, but as enforceable legal codes we lay them out thus.

violation of something important to breach that relationship between owner and owned. Perhaps it was my own desire to possess what was mine that instinctively told me that stealing was wrong. *"Do unto others what you would have them do unto you"*[120] is intuitive to many even if they choose against its quiet bleating.

When it came time to leave, the little guy was in that part of the cycle (no pun intended) where he was in my pocket. We cleaned up our mess as this little guy burned a hole in my soul. Will I take it? Will I put it back? I want it. It is wrong to take it. It's just a little thing. It's not mine. They probably don't even play with it anymore. It belongs to someone else.

My mother, carrying my little brother in one arm, took my hand and moved us all off the porch and through the yard back to our monstrosity of a dingy tan station wagon. I remember thinking even then how ugly it was. A 60s Chrysler Town & Country I believe.

The second I made the choice my whole life changed. I pulled my hand from my mother's and bolted back to the house as she called after me, a tad annoyed. I pulled that little guy out of my pocket and ran up the wooden steps and back onto the closed-in porch. I tossed it back into the toy box with a willful glee. I almost wondered if those around me heard it break… my heart certainly felt it break… the very temptation to steal.

Seriously! I have never even been tempted to steal another person's possessions as long as I have lived from that moment on. I want my due, yes. I want what I've earned, but I have no interest in taking another person's things. You could put a million dollars on a table and leave it unattended in my presence, and I would not feel the urge to take a dime of it even if I knew that its owner would never know.

Now, what really broke that day, was not theft. It turns out there are other drives behind theft than what broke that day, and I would face them in mortal combat later, but that day, a powerful form of covetousness died at the end of my spiritual sword… the sinful envy in craving for other people's things.[121]

Even now, however, after so many years dancing on its grave, the words of Paul come clearly to me from 1 Corinthians 10:12- 13, *"let anyone who thinks that he stands take heed lest he fall. No temptation has overtaken you that is not common to man."* Therefore, may the mirror of God's word expose those places where covetousness still reigns, even secretly, in all our hearts. Ask for God's help in killing it. There is great freedom in its demise.

Here is a prayer for the Christian. "Lord, teach my soul to be content with what I have. May the desire for improvement lead me not to covetousness, but to greater wisdom, industry and charity toward all."

~Andrew D. Sargent, Ph.D.

---

[120] Matthew 7:12.

[121] Runaway lust is another form of covetousness that demands its own personal war.

# Reflections & Responses

Coveting might not be a common word, but it certainly is useful in advertising... stir discontent, provoke envy, promise happiness in things. Considering Moses' general list of coveting in Exodus, make a more specific for yourself confessing the ways covetousness has struggled for control in your own soul.

As a counter to envy, make another list that takes inventory of all the good things God has allowed to grace your life. It can help to compare your blessing to what you have seen lacking in other places in the world.

Pray today and every day for God help you find gratitude for each good gift with which He has blessed you. It's hard to be upset about what we don't have, if we are too busy being grateful for what we do have.

# DAY THIRTY
## Weird Things Like Revelation & The Second Coming

It shouldn't be too long into joining a church that you hear something that strikes you as rather peculiar—The Second Coming of Jesus Christ… not to mention whispers of an equally peculiar book for which this events takes center stage—Revelation.

For pagans, who dominated the globe from earliest human memory, and Atheists, who are cooking up similar intentions of their own and are gaining ground, the human presence on the planet is purposeless and meaningless no matter how much joy we get from cat videos… or how much virtue we feel while picketing for an equal outcomes world. Why should you have more than me just because you work and produce and I spend my day watching cat videos?

Now, imagine the wonder of a person drowning in a pagan "reality," who opens the pages of Scripture and reads what is waiting for him there. There is One Holy God who made the world with a purpose and a plan. It tells the reader that he, along with all humans, has been assigned a special role in the fulfillment of that plan… God's special agents in Creation, filled with His Holy Spirit, walking in intimate communion with the Creator, knowing, known, loving and loved.

Imagine his grief when he reads how his forebears forsook this honor and rebelled against the Creator, dooming him to his present state. Yet, hope springs when he discovers that God has not wholly abandoned them, deserve it as they do. Rather the Lord has revealed a yet more amazing part of the plan—Man's redemption and restoration. Through the substitutionary atonement[122] provided by the Creator Himself, and his own repentance and obedience to the Maker's teaching,[123] God be praised, he can discover the path of life laid down in the created order and rejoin the mission of the ages, demanding as it is.

This mission has a beginning in millennia past. It has a trajectory in human history. It has epochs of growth, like the great flood, the calling of Abraham, the creation of Israel, the giving of Torah, the revelations of God's prophets, the coming of God's Messiah to redeem Mankind and establish His church. It also, shockingly enough, has a culmination, an end goal, a climax that leads to participation in some yet more glorious union and cooperation with God in the age which follows.

---

[122] I.e. Jesus died for other people's sins so that they could be saved from the consequences of that sin by becoming part of Jesus' new family.

[123] This is not to suggest that any act of man can earn his salvation, but rather that the full richness of life before God is enjoyed only by those who respond properly to God's gracious and salvific work on Man's behalf.

The prophetic books of the Old Testament cast repeated visions for this eventuality. The end is doom to those who perish in their sins, denying God His right of place or openly rejecting Him. It is eternal, abiding life for those who repent and believe. Some of these prophets wrote books called "Apocalyptic" literature which uses powerful images borrowed from the pagan world around Israel to speak powerfully about the Creator's eventual victory over all who make war against Him and against His people. They are weird... like really weird if you compare them to something like *Anne of Green Gables,* or even *the Gospel of Mark.*

Jesus is recorded in the biblical Gospels speaking of this plan several times,[124] like at the last supper before His arrest and crucifixion saying, "*I tell you I will not drink again of this fruit of the vine until that day when I drink it new with you in my Father's kingdom.*"[125] His return to bring the age of the earth to a close is promised by angels in Acts 1:10-11, "*And while they were gazing into heaven as he went, behold, two men stood by them in white robes, and said, "Men of Galilee, why do you stand looking into heaven? This Jesus, who was taken up from you into heaven, will come in the same way as you saw him go into heaven.*"

Peter boasted of the privilege of participating in the Church's stage of the divine plan, saying, "*He has caused us to be born again to a living hope through the resurrection of Jesus Christ from the dead, to an inheritance that is imperishable, undefiled, and unfading, kept in heaven for you, who by God's power are being guarded through faith for a salvation ready to be revealed in the last time.*"[126]

This event is also a primary point of discussion in a couple of the Apostle Paul's letters, like 2 Thessalonians 1:6-10, "*God considers it just to repay with affliction those who afflict you, and to grant relief to you... when the Lord Jesus is revealed from heaven with his mighty angels in flaming fire, inflicting vengeance on those who do not know God...when he comes on that day to be glorified in his saints, and to be marveled at among all who have believed.*"

The Second Coming of Christ is a core tenant of Christianity, declared "the Blessed Hope" by Paul, as he longs aloud, "*Looking for that blessed hope, and the glorious appearing of the great God and our Savior Jesus Christ, Who gave himself for us, that he might redeem us from all iniquity, and purify unto himself a peculiar people, zealous of good works.*"[127]

It is also, however, a source of more than a little controversy as we who believe strive to anticipate the details of the events that will "soon" come upon us.

The Coming of Jesus feels a lot sooner to me now than it did when, as a child, I imagined the events thought to be predicted in the pages of Scripture—

---

[124] Matthew 7, 16, 24, 25, 26, 28; Mark 13; Luke 8, 12, 17, & 21 etc.
[125] Matthew 26:29,
[126] 1 Peter 1:3-5
[127] Titus 2:13-14

150

like a one-world, God-hating government—impossible for my lifetime. Then we digitalized the world.

> *"Behold, he is coming with the clouds, and every eye will see him, even those who pierced him, and all tribes of the earth will wail on account of him. Even so. Amen. 'I am the Alpha and the Omega,' says the Lord God, 'who is and who was and who is to come, the Almighty.'"*[128] ...*"Behold, I am coming soon, bringing my recompense with me, to repay each one for what he has done."*[129]

~Andrew D. Sargent, Ph.D.

---

[128] Revelation 1:7–8
[129] Revelation 22:12

# Reflections & Responses

Write down your initial reaction to this devotional. Did is strike you as odd? Make you afraid? Give you joy? Explain.

Believing that you are an accident in an accidental world vs. believing that you have a purpose, a mission, and an end-goal affects the choices one makes in life. How did you perceive of your own existence before accepting Christ? Discuss some ways that this perception has changed.

The fact of Jesus' bodily return is basic Christianity. The exact details of the second coming of Christ, however, have been hotly debated. This provides us with a great opportunity... to have grace and charity with brothers and sisters in Christ, especially when we disagree about ambiguous things in Scripture... extra-especially when some don't know they are ambiguous.

# DAY THIRTY-ONE
## Christians Hope in the Face of Death

"I hope whoever speaks at this funeral doesn't get preachy and try to get a bunch of people saved. I hate when preachers do that at funerals. I don't get it, it's just *annoying*," says the rather confused woman to me at my Mother *and* Father-in-Law's funeral. Yes, both of my beloved in-laws passed away 3 days apart and we laid them to rest on February 14, 2020. Little did this woman know that *I was* that annoying preacher who would give the eulogy and call people to faith in Christ.

Why would I do that? Isn't it a put off... and off point? We are there to honor the lives of two dearly departed, isn't an "altar call" a distraction? Disrespectful?

Had she asked, I might have explained. I do this because nothing awakens us to eternity than a confrontation with death, and Christians prepare for eternity.

Our family has faced more than our fair share of loss. In one year, my husband and I attended 16 funerals of family, friends and loved ones. That was the year that our only dates nights were funerals. And the losses continued, parents, grandparents, aunts, uncles, friends. I have been awakened by an hysterical phone call that my aunt, a sister to me, was found dead on her bathroom floor. I have lain next to my grandmother hours before she passed. My uncle died in his sleep from unknown causes, which rocked our world with the fear that any one of us might simply never wake up. I have made final arrangements and put together celebration of life videos because other family members were just too shattered to help. So many eulogies.

More times than I can count, we have sat with those for whom the veil between the realms was paper-thin and watched them take their last breaths. One grandfather greeted his parents who had come for him, another talked with Jesus. He asked again and again to go home. When asked which home, he said, "I want to go home to be with Jesus." A little later I asked him, "What will you do first when you go home?" Expecting, "See my wife Roxie," I got, "I'm gonna praise God, praise God, praise God."

Every time we face another funeral, we do so knowing that there is more to this life than our years here on Earth. We know beyond a shadow of a doubt that death is not God's design for us. Indeed, most have a powerful sense that there is something wrong with the world, that death is not the plan, that there must be something else. Nothing makes us think more about what that could be than touching death.

Most people shy away from death and grieving. We want happy thoughts. It is uncomfortable to sit with the grieving; there is nothing we can say to help, nothing we can do to fix things. The grieving feel stuck in loss; the rest of the world goes on, but we can scarce imagine how to go on with it. So people distract themselves from uncomfortable emotions. They throw parties, play music, watch TV, work harder and longer, turn to substances to make us forget.

Ecclesiastes warns us about avoidance. It is better to go to a funeral than a party. People at funerals know that they will die and fix their soul on the reality of their future. Those who go to parties forget what's coming, and fail to prepare their souls. So 7:6 says, *"For as the crackling of thorns under a pot, so is the laughter of the fools,"* but 7:2 knows, *"It is better to go to the house of mourning than to go to the house of feasting, for this is the end of all mankind, and the living will lay it to heart."*

Christians know that death is not the end for us, if it were, Jesus, who went there, suffered that, and came back with the T-Shirt, would have told us. We trust God as the judge of all humanity to do right by our lost loved ones, and we hold onto Paul's promise in 1 Thessalonians 4:13-14, *"Brothers and sisters, we do not want you to be uninformed about those who sleep in death, so that you do not grieve like the rest of mankind, who have no hope. For we believe that Jesus died and rose again, and so we believe that God will bring with Jesus those who have fallen asleep in him."*

As we face death ourselves, we celebrate the example of Paul, who, sitting in prison, writes in Philippians 1:20-24 to tell believers, *"I eagerly expect and hope that I will in no way be ashamed, but will have sufficient courage so that now as always Christ will be exalted in my body, whether by life or by death. For to me, to live is Christ and to die is gain."*

Ok – let's stop here – to die is gain? How can death be gain?

I'm glad you asked! Christians live with conviction that when we die we will go to Christ where there is no more striving, and no need of "faith" for we shall know Him face to face.

Paul goes on to describe his longing in Philippians 1:22 saying, *"If I am to go on living in the body, this will mean fruitful labor for me. Yet what shall I choose? I do not know! I am torn between the two: I desire to depart and be with Christ, which is better by far; but it is more necessary for you that I remain in the body."*

For the Christian, when life is good or bad we have hope; when life as we know it ceases, we will be with Christ, and that is far better than any life we might live here on Earth. Here, now, we work for the Lord and waiting expectantly for the day He calls us to our true home with Him.

Just like my grandfather looking through the veil between the worlds knew which home he was going to, all of us who know Jesus as our savior are never truly alone whether here in the present or even in death. May we rejoice in the Lord always, in life, in death, and in everything in between.

~Amy Roberts Kinder, MA

# Reflections & Responses

Each of us will face death at some point in our lives. Whether it is the death of a loved one, or losing our own life here on earth – no one escapes it. Discuss how you thought about death before accepting Jesus. How has becoming a Christian changed this perception if at all.

How does inevitable death and final judgement before God motivate you to share the good news of God's saving grace with others?

Do you feel as Paul feels when he says, "to live is Christ and to die is gain?" Explain

Made in the USA
Columbia, SC
19 February 2025